Teacher Communication

Teacher Communication

A Guide to Relational, Organizational, and Classroom Communication

Ken W. White

ROWMAN & LITTLEFIELD
Lanham • Boulder • New York • London

Published by Rowman & Littlefield
A wholly owned subsidiary of The Rowman & Littlefield Publishing Group, Inc.
4501 Forbes Boulevard, Suite 200, Lanham, Maryland 20706
www.rowman.com

Unit A, Whitacre Mews, 26-34 Stannary Street, London SE11 4AB

British Library Cataloguing in Publication Information Available

Library of Congress Cataloging-in-Publication Data

Names: White, Ken W., 1950- author.
Title: Teacher communication : a guide to relational, organizational, and classroom communication /
   Ken W. White.
Description: Lanham : Rowman & Littlefield, [2016] | Includes bibliographical references and index.
Identifiers: LCCN 2016005906| ISBN 9781475828528 (cloth) | ISBN 9781475828535 (pbk.) | ISBN
   9781475828542 (electronic)
Subjects: LCSH: Communication in education. | Teacher-student relationships. | Teachers--Profes-
   sional relationships.
Classification: LCC LB1033.5 .W52 2016 | DDC 371.102/2--dc23 LC record available at https://
   lccn.loc.gov/2016005906

♾ ™ The paper used in this publication meets the minimum requirements of American
National Standard for Information Sciences Permanence of Paper for Printed Library
Materials, ANSI/NISO Z39.48-1992.

Printed in the United States of America

Contents

Preface

Relational pedagogy equips learners to become partners in their own education for life. —Ray Boyd, Neil MacNeill, and Greg Sullivan

This is the first edition of *Teacher Communication: A Guide to Relational, Organizational, and Classroom Communication*. It is written for all "teachers," including in-service and preservice, veterans and novices, and education students enrolled in various method and communication courses. It is a practical and readable resource for college classrooms and in-service teacher training sessions. Its purpose is to support teachers at any level in the achievement of their professional and career goals in a manner consistent with the integration of communication theory and practical application. *Teacher Communication* reflects principles of adult learning and applied problem-solving in the teaching process.

Teacher Communication offers a perspective on teacher communication generally outside the formal discipline of education. My PhD is in the area of speech communication, focused on instructional, organizational, and interpersonal communication. Many of the references in this book are from communication scholars interested in the communicative basis of teaching, particularly around organizations and relationships. The idea that schools and teaching can be improved by changing the social context of learning—organizationally and relationally—is a common thread that runs through the writings of many education reformers and scholars. Consequently, the book's general assertion is that teaching is improved in school organizations where there is strong community and enhanced relationships. Teaching issues like connectedness and the importance of relationships are permeating the educational agenda of the twenty-first century.

The book reflects Ernest L. Boyer's ideas in *Scholarship Reconsidered*. Boyer advances a new way of defining scholarship that balances theory with practice. He argues that scholarship has four equal, yet overlapping, professional functions: discovery, integration, application, and teaching. *Discovery* is closest to what is traditionally meant by research; *integration* is interpreting information for meaning; *application* uses that meaning in practical ways; and *teaching* communicates and shares meaning with others.

Teacher Communication offers scholarship in the spirit of Boyer's definition. First, it offers discovery based on traditional forms of research and on lived experience, introducing readers to important disclosures from formal inquiry and teaching experience. Each chapter contains information about communication attitudes, skills, techniques, and methods discovered through thirty-five years of study and teaching.

Second, it shares an interpretation of teaching research through themes and guiding principles. For example, the theme of relational communication is stressed and applied throughout the book to impress upon readers that a positive and supportive relationship between teacher and student is key to effective teaching.

Third, *Teacher Communication* applies theory to teaching practices. It helps readers apply the breadth of teacher communication ideas to the depth of challenges that confront all teachers—new or seasoned.

Fourth, it gives readers a basic level of information to construct a workable meaning in the classroom. It is not too technically oriented, and it neither covers all aspects of teacher communication nor cites all possible references on a subject. It refers to current online blogs and articles to show what practicing teachers are actually doing today. Finally, it explains key topics—teacher communication competence and effective learning relationships—essential to a teacher's ability to communicate effectively, to think humanely, and to engage students in today's classroom.

Ultimately, *Teacher Communication* recognizes the fundamental role of communication in teaching. But instead of seeing teaching as simply the transmission of information, it views it as inherently relational. Teachers and students co-create meaning through communication and relational pedagogy. The book encourages teachers to enter into a dialogue with students and parents. Although it appreciates that there are times and places for teacher-centered approaches, it stresses that teaching is essentially about actively co-constructing knowledge with students, parents, and others.

A relational perspective emphasizes the interplay between teaching and learning. There is not a distinct line between the two. It is not as simple as "teachers teach" and "students learn." Teaching and learning phenomena are emergent properties of the social organization and relationships in the classroom. Terms like *teaching* and *communication* are neither objective nor subjective but intersubjective attributes created in a social context where both teachers and students gain knowledge and skills. Teaching is a dynamic communicative process, one that is not reducible to simply sending and receiving information.

In other words, *Teacher Communication* goes beyond a solely message-centered approach to communication and teaching. It asks teachers to take responsibility for more than delivering content and to participate actively in the social foundation of learning. Relationships are the heart of learning. Learning is never solely a student obligation; it is a social event where students need to feel a sense of belonging in the classroom and where teachers need to depend less on showing authority and more on building community. Learning develops through positive teacher–student relationships, and positive teacher–student relationships develop through learning.

On the other hand, although relationships are the foundation of good teaching—students learn more effectively when they are partners in their own education—relationships are not enough. Without improved student learning, relationships do not make for good teaching. Effective teaching results in better student achievement and performance.

Helping teachers become more relational should also not reduce teaching to techniques or formulas. There is more to good teaching than simply following tips or rules. Effective teachers take responsibility for their own teaching, and they judge how communication concepts apply to their own situation and needs. Individual assessment of ideas and their possible application are necessary for taking full advantage of this book. For example, the book does not address any particular age or grade level of students. It requires imagination about how ideas might apply to specific circumstances. It is like in my course—Public Speaking for Educators—where I ask students to show this kind of imagination. Students read ideas intended for secondary or college instruction and are required to identify the essence of a communication concept or strategy. Then they apply that essence in a lesson plan intended for elementary learners. The activity always works. Students come up with creative ways to make ideas work in elementary settings. I hope readers do the same with this book.

OUTCOMES

Communication abounds in all areas of teaching. *Teacher Communication* is a straightforward guidebook to basic knowledge and skills that help teachers develop the necessary outcomes to communicate more effectively with students, parents, and colleagues. The outcomes include the following:

- attitudes and skills that help teachers respond effectively to aspects of relational, organizational, and classroom communication
- better teacher communication and improvement in the quality of communication as a whole
- a path to greater on-the-job satisfaction, performance, and success in teaching

These outcomes are supported throughout the book. Part I introduces a communicative perspective on teaching and relational communication. Chapter 1 describes a philosophical basis for teacher communication. Chapter 2 emphasizes the role of relational communication in teaching and sets the stage for a discussion of choice in teacher communication behaviors in chapter 3. Chapter 4 concludes with a way to develop teacher communication competence.

Part II provides readers with information on the role of communication within the social organization of teaching. Chapters 5 through 7 concentrate on the nature and structure of effective learning relationships and communicating with parents and principals. Chapter 8 focuses on how effective communication helps teachers to successfully handle conflict.

Part III addresses forms of classroom communication. Classroom communication for teachers entails dealing with group or team communication, making effective presentations, leading discussions, and communicating effectively online. Teacher Communication is written in a deliberatley colloquial tone. I want this book to be practical, usable, and accessible. My understanding of teaching and communication has been influenced by a number of traditions and philosophies. But I want the book to be immediately intelligible to teachers and students new to these traditions and philosophies. I hope it is.

Acknowledgments

I acknowledge that I am not an expert about teacher communication. I have studied it for over thirty years and taught it for about the same amount of time. But I know the difference between theory and practice. I continue to be a learner. I have had communication successes in schools and classrooms—with colleagues and students—and I have had setbacks. I find assurance in teaching "one day at a time," reflecting on communication successes and failures, and asking: What can I do better next time? I can only offer my experience, reflections, and responses to that question.

I also acknowledge people who contributed in direct and indirect ways to this book. My most important living relationships—with my wife, Holly, and my sons, Nathaniel and Jamieson—are the central reasons for continuing to learn and to write. I am grateful for Holly's assistance in reading numerous drafts and clarifying my thoughts and words as she does every day. She is my partner in all parts of my life.

I thank former professor and teacher John Stewart for inspiring my interest in the communicative and philosophical basis of teaching, and for introducing many of the ideas in this book. John's advice to "live within the tension" remains challenging and poignant.

I also thank my former high school history teacher at Cascade High School in Everett, Washington. Paul Trekeme taught me that teaching is an invitation to share a passion. His compassion was contagious. Finally, I thank readers who have communicated and motivated me to write this book. I invite comments about its practicality, readability, and philosophical approach. Please send any ideas or simply greetings to white_kenw@msn.com.

Ken White

I

Teaching and Relational Communication

Students are drawn toward teachers they trust and perceive as competent and caring. —*V. P. Richmond*

Teacher communication is about the roles communication plays in the classroom and how teachers can develop the ability to communicate competently in educational settings. Teachers communicate with a diversity of people—students, administrators, parents, and colleagues—and in a diversity of settings. In all of these situations, teachers face communication challenges: a student doesn't listen in class; a parent wishes to understand his or her child's academic difficulty; an administrator wants to discuss a student's problems in the classroom; and a fellow teacher complains about the problems with a "high stakes" testing environment.

Part I introduces the subject of teacher communication, particularly relational communication and teacher communication competence. Again, it is intended to be practical. Good theory is good practice. If one cannot translate theory into practical behaviors—into "cash value"—it is not good theory. Consequently, there is a direct relationship between ideas and practice in each chapter. Although it is challenging to make a direct relationship between general theory and specific practices of individual teachers, part I presents a way for readers to judge the usefulness of its ideas about teacher communication for themselves.

TEACHER COMMUNICATION AND PEDAGOGY

To begin, there are three major domains in the field of teacher communication: communication pedagogy, developmental communication, and instructional communication. *Communication pedagogy* is commonly defined as the principles and methods of teaching communication content. The word *pedagogy* has its roots in ancient Greece. Wealthy families had many servants and slaves, one of whom would be tasked to look after the children. Slaves would lead or escort the children to the place of education. The Greek word for child is *pais,* and the word for leader is *agogus.* A *pedagogue* was literally a leader of children. Later, the word *pedagogue* became synonymous with the teaching of our young. (Many contemporary educators describe the teaching of adults as *andragogy.*)

Communication pedagogy involves far more than simply transmitting information to learners or filling them up with knowledge. Effective pedagogy involves leading people to a place where they can learn for themselves. It is about creating learning environments and relationships where students can create their own knowledge, interpret the world in their own unique ways, and ultimately realize their full potential as human beings. It is about moving students.

Most important, communication pedagogy recognizes that all pedagogy is mediated through communication. Effective teaching and learning are dependent on the quality of communication between teacher and students. Of course, all teachers do not successfully communicate content in the classroom. They may not understand that a teacher's knowledge of content—*what* is communicated—is separate from whether he or she can make that content meaningful to students—*how* it is communicated. Leading and moving students depend on the nature of teacher—student communication. All teachers are faced with the challenges of communicating subject matter to students and engaging those students in the learning process.

The communication pedagogical perspective is about teaching content in ways that help students develop communicative understanding and skills. It emphasizes that effective teachers use multiple teaching strategies because there is no single, universal way that suits all learners. Diverse strategies are used in different combinations with different students to improve learning outcomes. Good pedagogy is about guiding diverse students to learning.

Teacher communication pedagogy addresses such questions as the following:

- What are the basic *functions* of communication?
- What are the different *models* of communication and what do they emphasize?
- What are the phases of *teacher communication competence*?
- What are the *differences* between impersonal and interpersonal communication?

All teachers are faced with these questions in their communication. How they respond to these questions determines what they believe about communication and how it affects their teaching.

TEACHING AND DEVELOPMENTAL COMMUNICATION

Developmental communication refers to the use of communication for individual and social development. Simply defined, developmental communication is when communication is used to promote human growth. It systematically applies the processes, strategies, and principles of communication to produce positive social interaction. It does this by improving communication skills, establishing effective learning environments, assessing communication attitudes and skills, and utilizing communication interventions to bring about productive behavioral, cognitive, and affective development in students.

Developmental communication programs provide services to students who are in need of developing and expanding their speech and/or language skills. These difficulties may occur alone or may be seen in conjunction with such diagnoses as global developmental delay, specific language impairment, autism spectrum disorder, Down syndrome, and Williams syndrome. Developmental techniques include tracking communication challenges like apprehension or anxiety across time, measuring how communication behaviors change, and focusing on the long-term impact of communication techniques and learning.

The developmental communication perspective is not as concerned with communication content as it is with how communication attitudes and skills develop over a period of time. For example, one goal of developmental communication is to ensure that students with delayed speech or language skills receive help early in school by stressing the importance of recognizing the warning signs as quickly as possible. The perspective emphasizes specific milestones in language development and communication that students are expected to reach by certain ages and advises that students who miss one or more of these milestones may need extra help to catch up.

Developmental communication addresses questions such as the following:

- What *classroom techniques* help students develop effective discussion skills?
- What role does communication play in the *development of relationships*?
- How can teachers address *communication apprehension*?
- How does productive *small group communication* develop and change over time?

Again, teachers face these communication concerns every day in the classroom. How they utilize resources and respond to these issues can determine how effectively they help students and themselves improve communication development over the long run.

TEACHING AND INSTRUCTIONAL COMMUNICATION

Instructional communication examines how communication promotes learning in a variety of teaching contexts, such as traditional classrooms, organizational training, and interpersonal skills preparation. It includes teacher-student interaction, teaching styles, student behaviors, and student outcomes. In other words, it is about how to use communication effectively to teach. Instructional communication is interested in the effect of teacher communication on learning, including the impact of mass media and online communication on student learning.

For example, instructional communication research has identified three distinct types of teacher concerns about communication—self, task, and impact. Teacher communication concern is a concept and research line developed to describe specific teaching behaviors that influence student learning. Beginning teachers are generally concerned with whether they have what it takes to be a teacher. Experienced teachers move on to being more concerned about mastering specific teaching skills and methods. Seasoned teachers, on the other hand, are most concerned about their long-term impact on student learning. The *communication concern construct* helps teachers understand that changes in their teaching behavior occur in direct relation to the changes in their communication concerns.

Instructional communication research established that there is no "best way" to communicate within a classroom. Instead, effective teacher communication attitudes and behaviors vary depending on the personalities and needs of the teacher, the types of students in the classroom, the congruence of teacher verbal and nonverbal messages, the level and quality of interaction among the teacher and students, and the larger effect on the classroom of the general communication climate of a school.

In early instructional communication research, communication was generally seen as flowing downward in classrooms, such as when teachers issue "commands." Communication was primarily message centered, and recommendations focused on teacher *clarity*, or *precision*. On the other hand, researchers came to recognize that communication is relational—effective teacher communication involves concepts such as teacher *immediacy*. Immediacy is a perception of a teacher's psychological closeness, friendliness, and approachability. Immediacy behaviors bridge the psychological gap between teachers and students and are linked to significant learning outcomes.

Today, instructional communication is seen as much more relationally centered. Teachers are involved in various types and levels of relationships that require different communication goals and behaviors, both message oriented and relationally oriented. A teacher in the physical education department who communicates with a teacher in the art department might have the message-centered goal of persuading colleagues about ideas for a different class scheduling policy, but the same PE teacher who communicates with the same art teacher might have the relationally centered goal of sharing frustrations and bonding about a school's reduced time for physical education and art.

Instructional communication research has identified three positive ways teachers relate to students through communication. First, teachers who practice supportive communication behaviors increase students' sense of belonging and affective learning. Second, teachers who build "classroom connectedness" and students' perceptions of positive communication climates help to improve school attendance and reduce bullying. Third, teachers who have knowledge about student backgrounds, experiences, and goals can better target instruction toward students' learning needs.

Instructional communication addresses questions such as the following:

- What teaching behaviors promote *teacher clarity*?
- How does *teacher immediacy* help to develop effective teacher—student relationships?
- How does *teacher credibility* promote effective relationships with colleagues, principals, and parents?
- What *questioning techniques* help teachers to facilitate effective classroom discussions?

Teachers face questions about instructional communication every day. How they respond to these questions can determine how effectively they use communication in their classrooms and how well students relate to the teacher, learning, and the school.

CONCLUSION

The chapters in part I help teachers see communication differently in order to develop the attitudes and skills for making effective communication choices. Chapter 1 introduces the area of teacher communication, the "command" function of communication, and ways to improve feedback and active listening. Chapter 2 moves beyond the area of command communication and stresses the importance of "relational" communication in productive teacher—student relationships. Although command communication is intentional, purposeful, and rational, the chapter argues that relational communication is nonintentional and teachers cannot NOT communicate.

Chapter 3 stresses that competent teacher communication is the result of the choices made when dealing with the uncertainties and ambiguities of relational communication. It argues that effective teacher communication is an outcome of better communication choices. Chapter 4 concludes with a model of teacher communication competence intended to help teachers develop and take control of their choices.

As the book moves from the general principles behind teacher communication to actual classroom communication practices, teachers should keep in mind that getting the most out of this book requires

- an openness to learning and trying new ideas, and
- the mindfulness that teaching is a way of communicating.

Being open to learning doesn't mean having to believe everything in this book. It simply means that readers must become aware of how past ideas and experiences (what is referred to as the "horizon of experiences") can interfere with their openness to different communication ideas. To be open is not to be gullible; it is to be thoughtful.

Teaching as a way of communicating means that readers are willing to engage and apply the communication ideas in this book to their own teaching. Readers need to "try on" the behaviors and appreciate that the quality of teaching is determined by the quality of communication. If teachers want to improve their teaching, they need to think about their communication. The ideas, tips, and techniques presented in this book are only as good as the willingness and mindfulness of readers.

ONE

Teacher Communication

The difference between knowing and teaching is communication.
—*H. T. Hurt, M. D. Scott, and J. C. McCroskey*

Effective communication is an essential part of teaching. A teacher's communication skills can be a decisive factor in success or failure in critical teaching situations. That is why many teachers place high value on communication skills. They see proficient communication as a requirement for teaching effectively, coping with conflict, motivating learners, making decisions, leading students, and facilitating important human relations skills. Communication is the cornerstone of great instruction.

Unfortunately, confusion about what is appropriate and inappropriate communication in various educational contexts is also common. For example, one can find plenty of teachers perplexed about social media. As teachers' social roles become more entangled in online technology, it becomes harder to distinguish private from personal concerns. Mike Simpson, assistant general counsel of the National Education Association (NEA), has observed that many teachers believe they have the absolute First Amendment right to post anything they want on Facebook and other social media sites. This is a serious problem for young teachers with an electronic trail who are looking for their first job.

Confusion is understandable in light of the complexity associated with contemporary teacher communication, especially if teaching is seen simply as the transmission of information and messages. This chapter presents a functional definition of communication relevant to instructional contexts as offered by Charles Conrad, a noted organizational communication scholar. Conrad defines communication as the process through which people issue, receive, interpret, and act on commands. His approach helps teachers create and maintain productive communication with other members of school organizations, especially students and colleagues. Before proceeding with the implications of Conrad's two-fold definition, a brief look at the complexity of communication and why a functional approach is useful to teachers is in order.

THE FUNCTIONS OF TEACHER COMMUNICATION

Communication is defined differently across disciplines and possesses many meanings. Seeking a single working definition of this term is not as productive as identifying its functional components. The concept of communication functions legitimately in a number of ways. Although it is a problem to define the term precisely, it is beneficial to ask how communication functions as forms of teacher behavior. Charles Conrad (2012) identifies two functions relevant to teaching:

- The command function
- The relational function

Conrad defines *command communication* as any message that influences other people—students, parents, colleagues, or administrators—to take action or to accept certain ideas. A command is not necessarily an order. It can also be a statement, question, or request. The following section discusses the command function of teacher communication and its dependence on effective feedback and active listening. The chapter concludes with some observations on the limitations of command communication. Chapter 2 then turns to the relational aspect of teacher communication.

THE COMMAND FUNCTION OF TEACHER COMMUNICATION

The command function reveals that teachers communicate effectively at one level when they initiate and limit actions in clearly prescribed ways. This is teacher *clarity*. From this perspective, communication begins when a teacher attempts to transmit information to another person. This is likened to the popular *message-centered model of communication*. A teacher sends messages in order to have students take certain actions and limit those actions to a particular series of steps. The transmission is conscious, rational, and expressed through oral instructions and written assignments.

Oral instructions are messages or commands given in face-to-face encounters and usually addressed to a single student or a clearly identified group of students, such as when a teacher monitors group projects. Oral instructions are flexible and transient rather than permanent. They are linked to specific problems that are relatively new, rare, or unprecedented. For example, if assigning group presentation where education students are required to teach other students how to apply educational frameworks in teaching, students may not be familiar with the term *framework*. So when students are planning in their groups, it is helpful for the teacher to give oral instructions about how to identify an educational framework. Oral instructions can vary from group to group depending on the prior knowledge a group shows about the subject.

In contrast, written assignments or publications are general commands to a whole classroom. The written message is addressed to any and every student, and it makes the command official. Publications are written by the teacher in a formal capacity. They are relatively permanent injunctions and, indirectly, address problems that are important and recurring. Building on the above example, written assignments on educational frameworks can be given to all students and groups to introduce them to the presentation. Written messages outline formal requirements in class and are starting points for individual student understanding.

Message-Centered Model of Teacher Communication

Regardless of the particular communication channel, the command perspective begins with a perception—a thought or a feeling—that must be encoded as a message before it is transmitted. Encoding involves putting a message "into a code." When teachers send messages either as written or oral instructions, students decode and transform the messages into perceptions or interpretations. Student interpretations must be clarified by the oral instructions of the teacher. Figure 1.1 represents the basic message-centered, or interactive, process.

The message-centered model of communication is simple and direct but can be misleading. Understanding the simplest message can be hampered because many elements of the communication process are inherently private and not shared (e.g., thoughts and feelings, encoding, decoding). Of course, a teacher's command functions more effectively if students provide feedback and the teacher listens to that feedback. Useful feedback clarifies interactive communication whenever a student responds to the original message of the teacher by asking a question or expressing a lack of understanding.

The hidden elements of communication indicate that it is not only words that are transmitted and received in communication. Something else is at work. Sometimes feedback is not sufficient to address this something else. Often it is the way words are interpreted—what lenses or filters of meaning people use to decode them. When these lenses are at work, people may not even be aware of their existence.

Consequently, it is necessary to add an important feature to the basic message-centered model of communication in order for it to more accurately represent how people use perceptual lenses to interpret messages. The German philosopher and educator Hans-Georg Gadamer (1989)

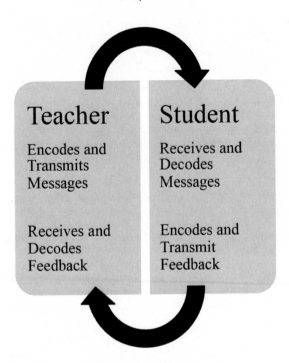

Figure 1.1.   Message-Centered or Interactive Model of Teacher Communication.

adds the idea of *horizons of experience* (p. 245). Horizons of experience are hidden aspects of human communication that influence and confound the achievement of individual meaning. It is all that can be perceptually realized by a person at a given time and setting, or the limits of how much a teacher or student can see or understand something. The concept offers a way to reconceptualize the process of teacher communication and deepen it.

Teachers and students initiate communication under the influence of horizons of experience. In particular, horizons of experience include what Gadamer calls *prejudices*—perceptions, values, biases, attitudes, experiences, and opinions that initiate interpretations of words and the world. The term *prejudice* is used by Gadamer to indicate presuppositions that set limits to interpretation, not just to carry racial connotations as popularly perceived. According to Gadamer (1989), prejudices are often negative or hidden, but not always. Prejudices can be positive. A student inclination to be a teacher is a prejudice, just a productive one as generally accepted. But hidden prejudices, whether positive or negative, are always part of horizons, inevitably distort understanding, and can dominate the perceptions and communication of people if not recognized and addressed (p. 270).

Gadamer's concepts of horizons of experience and prejudices show how communication is never completely objective for either students or teachers (p. 302). Everyone has horizons of experience that influence everything they perceive and are unique vantage points of experience and understanding. Both teachers and students have vantage points and "see," or understand, only as far as their horizons permit. This is the source of one possible breakdown in teacher–student communication. If either a teacher or a student sticks blindly to their horizons, fully understanding each other's messages is not possible.

Consequently, the command function and its message orientation are vulnerable to the inherent limitations of hidden factors like horizons and prejudices. Effective communication depends on a teacher recognizing the role these factors play in communication. Teachers cannot communicate effectively without understanding how horizons and prejudices, particularly their own, influence all interactions and meaning. It is necessary for teachers to have some sense of where they and their students are coming from, and what prejudices may be influencing the interpretation of messages.

Misunderstanding occurs partly because of the challenge teachers and students face in going beyond apparent words and acknowledging each other's hidden horizons, prejudices, feelings, and personal experiences. Gadamer argues that responding to communication's limitations requires relating interpersonally (p. 250). In other words, effective teacher communication needs to be relational. It needs more than precision and clarity. It needs reading between the lines and connecting to another person's horizon. For example, a student's anger in class may be the result of past experiences with another teacher's misuse of authority, resulting in the student perceiving and stereotyping all teacher authority as illegitimate. If the teacher is sensitive to this possibility and knows the student's background and experiences, he or she can get beyond the words and expressions of anger to a fuller relational understanding. The teacher can adjust his or her communication to show more immediacy, approachability, and friendliness and attempt to counterbalance the defensive mood of the student.

Awareness of horizons of experience, prejudices, and relational communication offers teachers a way to communicate differently than simply by technical or command-centered means. Teacher communication benefits from a teacher's ability to sense a student's vantage point and to adjust communication accordingly. Recognizing student horizons of experience and prejudices requires more relational communication in the classroom. Teachers can communicate differently depending on how they relate to students.

To summarize, the command function of communication (or the message-centered model) reminds teachers that effective communication requires conscious and logical steps. Communication is partly a technical tool—we get things done with it. For example, teachers need to communicate a time and place in order for meetings to happen. But relational elements cannot be ignored. If teachers want to understand the complexity of communication, and communicate more effectively with students, parents, and colleagues, they need to recognize the importance of horizons of experience and prejudices. These concepts must be added to any description of command communication to accurately represent the complex dynamics of teacher communication. Those dynamics include the following:

- Encoding—a thought or idea put into a verbal or nonverbal code and transmitted to another person.
- Transmitting—a physical act of sending a message by vocal cords, mouth, or nonverbal means.
- Receiving—a physical act of hearing a verbal or nonverbal message.
- Decoding—a process of perceiving and making sense of a verbal or nonverbal message.
- Feedback—interpretation of how a verbal or nonverbal message has been received.
- Horizons of experience—a perceptual limitation of how far a person can see or understand something.
- Prejudices—perceptions, values, biases, attitudes, experiences, and opinions that filter a person's meaning of verbal and nonverbal messages.

It is clear that the logic and precision of command communication does not reflect the full richness of teacher communication or account for its relational dynamics. A reconceptualized model of teacher communication is necessary. Figure 1.2 represents a contextualized, or enhanced, description of a message-centered communication process where horizons of experience and prejudices filter the other elements of command communication and where messages are equally exchanged and interpreted. Words alone are not enough to achieve meaning and understanding. Like an onion, communication and understanding are layered. The creation of meaning moves through horizons of experience and prejudices to the encoding and decoding of messages. Teachers need to actively listen to students to understand the hidden interpretations filtered through the students' horizons of experience and prejudices.

Listening to Student Feedback

Although teachers must go beyond command communication to be effective in the classroom, it is not necessary to throw out the baby with the bathwater. The command perspective is beneficial and offers useful suggestions for improving the clarity of teacher communication. In order

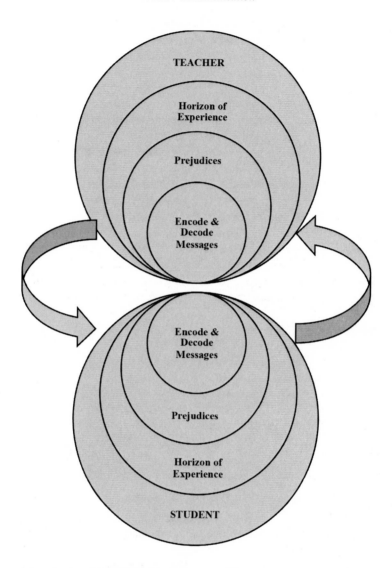

Figure 1.2. Contextualized Message-Centered Model of Teacher Communication.

for command communication to function effectively and for messages to be clear, teachers require adequate feedback from students. Teachers can assume that their students will simply carry out their commands—an assumption especially strong when the teacher has issued a set of written instructions—but adequate student feedback is necessary to show that students may be coming from a completely different perspective. Teachers can believe that their commands will be carried out, and they can instruct students for the task to be accomplished, but students might still fail to carry out the commands successfully. Listening to prompt and accurate student feedback allows teachers to modify commands and help students succeed at the task.

As figure 1.2 implies, communication requires timely and appropriate *active listening* on the part of the teacher in order to achieve understanding with a student. In situations where students do not give feedback, or where teachers do not actively listen to that feedback, students are unable to articulate important questions or clarify a teacher's intent. The teacher cannot add to the student's interpretation. As a result, students do not understand the material and the teacher is unaware of students' lack of understanding.

The command function requires student feedback to improve teacher communication. Feedback is an opportunity to correct and refine communication and to produce mutual understanding and agreement. Feedback should be encouraged whenever teacher communication functions to transmit commands. Teachers improve the effectiveness of their commands by encouraging two-way communication and actively soliciting student feedback.

Two listening techniques that improve two-way communication and help teachers acquire important student feedback are *paraphrasing* and *perception checking*. Paraphrasing and perception checking are active listening skills. Active listening enhances teacher understanding by clarifying student meaning and encouraging more thorough student feedback. Teachers support command communication and improve the quality of feedback when they engage in the following communication techniques.

Practice Paraphrasing

Paraphrasing attempts to restate a student's message. Though not parroting, a teacher repeats back the meaning of a student's words. Different working interpretations in communication, labeled as *horizons of experience* and *prejudices* in figure 1.2, make it hard to understand a message, particularly a long or complex one. The objective of paraphrasing is to ensure that the teacher gets the sense of a student's understanding.

A good paraphrase is concise and involves key words. When teachers begin to paraphrase—such as writing down student responses to a discussion on the board—they are often too wordy. If there are too many words, the message gets lost. When leading discussions, for example, teachers want to correctly reflect student comments. A good paraphrase summarizes the student's message, cuts through the clutter, and focuses on the essence of the student's ideas. This helps teachers develop a sense of what is key or central to a student's message.

Effective paraphrasing can also help teachers understand the emotional content of a student's message. Emotion is always part of communication, and when one is trying to paraphrase a message, it is productive to deal with the underlying emotions of the message rather than just the facts. By including the emotional content of a message, teachers can develop a more comprehensive understanding of the student's frame of reference.

Check Perceptions

Perception checking is similar to paraphrasing but more strongly focused on feelings. It intentionally checks out the emotions that motivate a student's communication. The concern isn't as much with what the student communicated (words) as much as it is with how the student conveys (tone) those words.

Teachers frequently overlook many of the emotional dimensions of student communication. They miss the student's vantage point and personal reaction to a topic being discussed. As philosopher William James put it, "Individuality is found in feelings" (Pruiott, 2016). If teachers miss the feelings, they miss the opportunity to sense the unique perspective of each student. Student emotions help teachers sort out information, organize it, and use it effectively as they listen and understand relevant feedback.

For example, if a student consistently comes to class late, a teacher might assume from this nonverbal communication that the student doesn't care much about his or her learning. If the teacher checks out this perception, he or she might find that the student cares greatly about school and learning but is affected and frustrated by outside events. Understanding a feeling of frustration in the student can lead the teacher to see the problem as associated with work or family tensions.

CONCLUSION

Command is not the only function of communication, and communication is never as simple as transferring information from one person to another. The process of teacher communication involves much more than mechanics, and it is virtually impossible to be trouble-free. When commands are not interpreted the "correct" way, it can be frustrating. For teachers, questions like "What's the right way?" may be less productive than asking, "What are my other choices?" "What can I do better?" In other words, effective communication is not simply a matter of good techniques—the correct way—but a matter of relating to individuals and their unique horizons of experience and prejudices.

Meanings are in people, in their horizons of experience and prejudices, not just in their words. Words have definitions but they do not *have*
meanings. People have meanings. One can go to the dictionary and look
up a word's various definitions, but the dictionary never understands the
unique intent of a person using the word. Words get us into the ballpark
of meaning, but we do not get meaning from the words alone. People,
including teachers and students, often give their own spin, if not meaning, to words. They attribute meanings based on their frames of reference
or vantage points. Teacher communication is a two-way process where
simply saying something correctly to another person is not the whole
story. It is a process of understanding students and their horizons of
experience.

Many day-to-day communication choices that teachers make in the
classroom are influenced by how teachers see communication—its connection to perceptions, experiences, feelings, and relationships. If teachers think communicative meaning is primarily in words or symbols, they
see communication as a matter of precision or correct grammar. But if
teachers see meaning as the sharing of horizons and the relationships
between people, communication becomes much more than the definitions of words. The next chapter addresses how teacher communication
is also about attitudes and emotions. It goes beyond command- and
message-centered communication and turns directly to the role of relational communication in teaching.

TWO

Relational Communication

One cannot NOT communicate. —*Joseph DeVito*

Chapter 1 discussed how communication helps teachers to perform necessary tasks by effectively initiating action through commands and by limiting those actions in clearly prescribed ways through feedback. In addition, the chapter presented command communication as the combination of a number of different components. To summarize, teacher command communication involves the following:

- Written instructions, or publications, address students or a classroom generally, and formalize a command. They are also the starting point for student understanding.
- Oral instructions, or explanations, address a single student or group of students and are linked to specific questions or problems at the time.
- Oral command instructions vary from student to student depending on prior knowledge.

Through the command function of communication, teachers transmit information to students for the rational completion of tasks. Teachers give commands effectively only when they encourage prompt and accurate student feedback. Precision, clarity, and feedback are central to command communication.

On the other hand, chapter 1 also introduced the concept of horizons of experience and prejudices. If teachers want to understand the complexity of command communication, they need to take into account some of its relational aspects, or lenses of interpretation, that affect teacher communication. This chapter looks more directly at how effective teacher communication requires teachers to rely on relational communication. To better explain the less rational world of relational communication

17

in teacher communication, it details the dual nature of teacher communication.

THE DUAL NATURE OF TEACHER COMMUNICATION

You probably played a game in school where you whispered a message into the ear of a friend. The friend would then repeat the message to another friend, and so forth. The process would be repeated down a long line of kids. You might recall that a message such as "The rain in Spain falls mainly on the plain" would end up as something like "A crane fell in the lane when hit by a plane."

The challenges of teacher communication are similar to this childhood game. Teacher communication involves not only the rationality of command communication but also the uncertainty and ambiguity of relational communication. One way to introduce the concept of relational communication is to look at formal and informal communication and their relation to open and closed communication in school organizations.

Formal School Communication

Formal school communication is vertical, either downward or upward, communication. For example, administrators, such as principals, give directives or information to teachers about the school organization or classroom environment. It is the relaying of official or formal messages. As downward, it transmits information from school leaders to teachers through speeches, bulletins, policy manuals, and procedure handbooks. The purposes of formal communication are to implement goals, strategies, and objectives; to offer instructions for job-related tasks; to share information regarding school practices and procedures; to give teacher performance feedback; and to create a common sense of purpose or community in the school.

As upward, formal communication is feedback from teachers designed to keep administrators in touch with what is happening. It helps administrators to determine if teachers have understood information sent downward. Upward communication includes messages to make administrators aware of difficulties, suggestions for school improvement, department or division performance reports, union grievances or disputes, and financial information.

Problems with formal communication are typically associated with barriers to effective upward communication in a school. Administrators fail to respond to upward information or are defensive about the information they receive. Although there are means for improving upward communication, such as administrative open-door policies or teacher group decision-making processes, open-door policies are seldom used, and group decision-making processes are only as effective as the willingness of teachers who participate. Teachers are often reluctant to pass on negative information to administrators. If giving negative feedback has no formal or objective channels or is stressful, teachers avoid giving it. They hide their negative thoughts and feelings. As a result, this tendency, known as the MUM effect, obstructs administrators from addressing important problems, and school performance may go in a wrong direction.

With poor upward communication teachers can become dependent on the grapevine to express bottled-up feelings. Like anyone else, teachers need to talk about what is affecting them, and if no official channels work, or they are not safe, the grapevine allows this kind of expression. In the grapevine, teachers can communicate using ordinary language instead of the bureaucratic jargon of formal communication channels. The breadth and depth of the grapevine can be a solid indicator of the health, morale, and productivity of a school.

Informal School Communication

No formal school document portrays the informal organization and its communication, as this aspect of the organization is influenced by informal political ties and friendships. While formal communication aids in the dissemination of official information, informal communication helps teachers to make sense of school dynamics and to express feelings, either implicitly or explicitly.

As mentioned above, the grapevine is an example of an informal communication channel that exists, to one degree or another, in all school organizations. The grapevine stems from teachers' need to work out emotions, and ultimately to make sense of what is happening to and around them. Surprisingly, information from the grapevine can be very accurate, but its main purpose is to be an emotional "escape valve" for school tensions as a result of considerable change.

The grapevine also carries unreliable information such as rumors. It is very difficult for administrators to combat rumors, so they are often tempted to overlook the grapevine. But the grapevine must be acknowledged because of the extent to which it influences the performance of a school. A large percentage of communication in the grapevine is true; but it is often difficult for administrators to separate fact from fiction. However, grapevine information gives administrators the opportunity to address and correct inaccuracies, falsehoods, and faulty communication processes. Without acknowledgment, the grapevine can simply fuel anxiety, conflict, and misunderstanding.

The grapevine can also reinforce teachers avoiding communication — again, the MUM effect. Consequently, it becomes even more challenging for administrators to assess the actual state of affairs in a school. Without productive paths of official communication, gossip and unconfirmed reports become more significant. The productivity and satisfaction of teachers is even more hampered if they do not have an opportunity to communicate within formal channels. The overdependence on the grapevine or the MUM effect leads to lack of communication with administrators. This impedes goodwill in a school and increases negative information and feelings about administrators.

Open and Closed Communication

The direction of information is a very important part of the school organization. Administrators and teachers must communicate effectively for a school to perform well. But there is another communication duality at work that is possibly more fundamental than formal and informal communication: open and closed communication (figure 2.1). *Open communication* occurs when all parties in a school are able to express ideas to one another. *Closed communication* occurs when the communication flow is determined mainly by one person.

In an open communication environment, teachers feel heard. In a meeting with an administrator to discuss a new process, they also reach a desired outcome. The administrator feels confident that teachers understand the new process. In a closed communication environment, teachers can feel unheard or even ignored. They leave a meeting with an administrator about a new process not knowing what the process is. Closed communication is when teachers feel that they have not reached a desired outcome.

The important point is that the communication environment of a school—open or closed—may indicate how administrators use formal and informal communication techniques. If administrators favor an open approach, formal communication usually involves more consistent information, feedback, and teacher participation in decision-making. But if administrators favor closed communication, there is often a lack of information, and teachers depend more on the informal communication of the grapevine.

Open or closed communication affects the coordination of meaning that needs to occur within both formal and informal communication processes. Both need to be utilized in order to increase effective school communication and to address problems and challenges. School administrators who favor open communication are better able to successfully integrate formal with informal communication and minimize the negative impacts of the grapevine.

THE RELATIONAL FUNCTION OF TEACHER COMMUNICATION

The dynamics of informal school communication make teacher communication considerably more challenging than simply dealing with official "commands." Communication in school organizations is not always rational or a carefully planned combination of interrelated and objective components. It is made up of living, thinking, and emotional human beings—actors who constantly make choices, not inanimate objects in a lifeless organization.

Thus teacher communication is not solely command-oriented but is also a medium for relational communication. In the relational realm, perceptions, horizons of experience, prejudices, and emotions—not tasks, commands, or logical sequences—provide significant factors within which teachers communicate. As a result, teachers require a tolerance for uncertainty. Instead of depending on communication clarity and precision, relational communication requires working with uncertainty and interpretations. If teachers adjust to a less rational process, relational communication can be an avenue for more effective communication and give meaningful structure to confusing and ambiguous information and situations.

Teachers who understand relational communication and its uncertainties are able to seek out information that creates useful perspectives

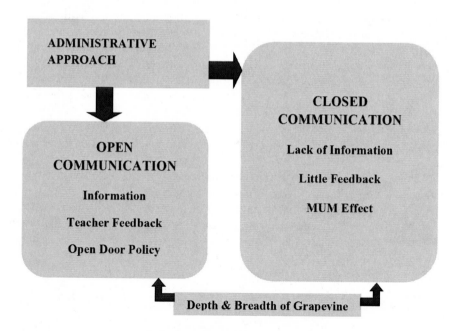

Figure 2.1. Open and Closed School Communication.

on challenges or problems. They get support from other teachers who confirm or disconfirm their interpretations and strengthen their commitment to a preferred action. Relational communication helps teachers create shared understandings of problems and reach consensus about how to address challenges. Teachers not only need sufficient, relevant, and accurate information, they need relational communication to improve decision-making.

Relational communication helps teachers make sense of—not control—the actions of others and coordinate those actions. Recognizing relational dynamics leads to understanding and accepting how humans think, communicate, organize, and act when contextualized by uncertainty. Martin Heidegger (1971) identifies this context as the *house of being* (p. 5). The house of being is language and communication with all of the ambiguity, vague words, and mixed messages that entails. Steven Piantadosi (2012) of the Massachusetts Institute of Technology argues that ambiguity actually makes language more efficient and is an essential part of communication. If communication and relationships are simply seen as tools to influence, manipulate, or control others and not as the lived experience of being with others, then teacher communication—formal or informal—falters.

One Cannot NOT Communicate

While command communication requires teacher communication to be intentional, purposeful, and rationally motivated, relational communication requires no such intention and is often emotionally motivated. To help teachers understand the difference, nonverbal communication is an excellent example. Imagine seeing students sitting in the back of your classroom with expressionless faces, perhaps staring at the front of the room or out the window. The students would probably say that they are not communicating attitudes or moods but they are "communicating" a great deal to you—disinterest, boredom, and desire for class to be over as soon as possible. The students are communicating, whether they think so or not.

On the other hand, imagine students seeing you in the front of the room with an expressionless face, perhaps staring at the ceiling or down at your desk. Although you may not believe that you are communicating with students at that moment, you can be communicating a great deal—disinterest, boredom, and desire for class to be over. You are communicating, whether you think so or not.

Nonverbal communication illustrates that communication is inevitable, whether people intend it or not. Teachers cannot control all that they are communicating. As Joseph DeVito (1999) declares, "One cannot NOT communicate." As a result, a crucial issue for teachers is how they can influence their effects within the uncertainty and inevitability of relational communication. Teachers can make "commands" clear and more precise to encourage understanding but cannot control all aspects of relational communication. But teachers can have a positive influence. The following examples of nonverbal communication illustrate the increased complexity of relational communication and the possibilities for positive interactions.

Kinesics of Body Language

Kinesics, or body language, includes a gamut of nonverbal cues: eye contact, body posture, facial expression, gestures, and body movement. It is a highly speculative field and difficult to define, but there is no question about its importance: the *way* a message is sent is often more relevant than *what* is said. Albert Mehrabian (1972) observes that a significant portion of communication is expressed without words. Meaning is expressed by facial gestures, posture, vocal intonation, and inflection. In fact, a smaller part of meaning might be verbal, though that is debatable.

The research is clear: judgments about visual cues are often more valid than judgments about vocal communication. In the classroom, when verbal and nonverbal messages differ, students tend to trust the nonverbal messages. To students, judgments of visual cues are more trustworthy than judgments based on vocal cues. Consequently, the importance of nonverbal communication and kinesics in teacher communication needs to be emphasized. Nonverbal behaviors and body language have a significant impact on student perceptions.

Describing teachers' positive nonverbal behavior in general terms is not difficult. The difficulty lies in specifics about which nonverbal behaviors or body movements are effective under which conditions and which are not. Take eye contact, for instance. Under most circumstances, making eye contact is positive nonverbal behavior. However, too much eye contact makes people feel uneasy. To fix someone with a cold stare is usually a sign of hostility. In addition, eye contact acceptable by Western standards can be perceived as rude by other cultures (e.g., Japanese). The same thing can be said for hand gestures and body movements.

Researchers know that body movements enhance the meaning of verbal messages. Ekman and Friesen (1967) found that facial features communicate feelings but body movements reveal how intensely people experience those feelings. If a student makes a face of frustration while trying to solve a math problem, he or she needs assistance with the content. But if the student pushes the desk away and physically moves away, he or she is extremely frustrated and needs assistance with attitudes. Learning to gauge feelings and intensity takes time and patience, but a teacher's attention to body movement and intensity improves the ability to facilitate effective learning relationships (to be discussed in chapter 5).

Other general observations and recommendations about body language benefit teachers. First, it is impossible to avoid communicating through body movement. As observed, *one cannot not communicate*. Everything teachers say or do—or are—sends a message. It might not be the message a teacher *intends* but it will have an *impact* on students. It is important for teachers to see the difference between what they intend with a message and what impact the message has on students. Teachers are always communicating and students are always interpreting.

Second, body language, along with voice intonation and inflection, is sometimes more important than the words teachers speak. All teacher communication is embedded in a nonverbal context. The key to effective teacher communication is sensitivity to the nonverbal environment. Teachers can periodically conduct personal sensitivity audits to better understand what their nonverbal communication might be saying. For example, when lecturing or sharing information, teachers can look to see if students are fidgeting, looking bored, or nodding with approval. Are they making direct eye contact, or looking disinterested? Communication needs to be adjusted depending on the audit. If students seem bored during a lecture, it helps a teacher to stop talking and have students create "buzz groups" in which they briefly discuss an issue from the lecture and report their findings to the class. The teacher can then resume the lecture with more attentive students.

Additionally, when conducting sensitivity audits, teachers should consider whether their verbal and nonverbal messages are generally congruent. Do a teacher's verbal messages match their nonverbal messages? Do nonverbal behaviors reflect the words? Congruence between verbal and nonverbal communication helps clarify communication and increase student engagement and understanding.

Third, teachers should audit the nonverbal communication of others—students, colleagues, and parents—so they can respond appropriately. Active listening skills are necessary to "check out" nonverbal cues emanating from others. For example, if a student yawns in class, it might be more productive for the teacher to avoid immediately perceiving the behavior as negative. Instead, the teacher can check out the action by observing, "Ralph, it looks like you're bored or tired today." Ralph then has the opportunity to respond, telling the teacher that he stayed up all night anxious about a job interview this weekend. Ralph isn't bored then he's tired and distracted.

Proxemics or Spatial Relations

Another area of nonverbal communication important for teacher communication is *proxemics*, or spatial relations—the study of the way people use space. Edward T. Hall (1963) indicates there are two main aspects of space: territorial and personal. Drawing on anthropology, Hall identifies four distinct distances: intimate, personal, social, and public. These distances range from skin contact of eighteen inches for intimate encounters to twelve feet and beyond for public distance.

A major implication of proxemics for teachers is the effect personal distance has on students and parents. Most teacher communication takes place in a "social distance" that ranges from four to twelve feet. "Personal distance," eighteen inches to four feet, is often employed in more interpersonal settings. As with other nonverbal communication, it is difficult to control or set rules for maintaining personal space. But the effect of personal distance should be factored into the sensitivity audit described above (e.g., "Am I too close?" "Should I back off?" "Is personal distance appropriate in this setting with this student or parent?").

A related concern pertains to touch. Touching, outside of incidental contact and handshakes (as part of a mutually understood greeting ritual), is always intimate. Sometimes it is appropriate outside of class to slap a colleague on the back or touch a student's arm to emphasize a point. For the most part, however, at least in Western culture, teachers should avoid touching students as part of their interpersonal communication repertoire, except to reciprocate an appropriate hug when initiated by a student.

Another application of proxemics regards open versus closed office or classroom design. An office or classroom with an open design typically has the desk and chairs aligned so that there are no physical barriers between those sitting in the office or classroom. Conversely, offices or classrooms with closed designs typically place a desk or other furniture between the teacher and students. Students tend to feel more welcome and comfortable in offices and classrooms with an open design compared with offices and classrooms with closed designs. They view teachers with an open design as being more immediate, friendlier, and helpful. Consequently, many teachers favor open office design—with the door ajar—because such a design facilitates better relational communication.

Chronemics or Temporal Relations

Chronemics, or temporal relations, is the study of how people use and perceive time. Tom Bruneau (1990) at Radford University has spent a lifetime investigating how time interacts in communication and culture. Bruneau observes that in Western society, time is often considered equal to money. In addition, speed—as an indicator of time—is also highly prized in some societies. In other cultures, there may be great respect for slowing down and taking a more long-term view of time.

Time is often an overlooked element in nonverbal communication. But it is particularly important in teacher communication. Teachers set dates for the completion of assignments and projects, schedule parent meetings, and, if part of union discussions, negotiate professional working hours, including coffee and lunch breaks.

Many schools develop formal and informal standards for the use of time by teachers and administrators. For example, it might be expected that teachers never arrive late for a meeting or an appointment with an administrator or parent, but it can be acceptable for a principal to arrive a little late or keep a teacher waiting. Such standards are a part of important organizational information and need to be recognized.

The importance of timing in teacher communication will be discussed later in a chapter on online communication. At this point, it is sufficient to say that attitudes toward time are communicated by the ways teachers deal with it.

CONCLUSION

As the last two chapters have discussed, the purpose of teacher communication is two-fold:

- To transmit commands as clearly and accurately as possible in order to achieve productive levels of understanding, and
- To maintain positive relationships with students, parents, and administrators.

Following are final reminders for improving teacher relational communication:

- Appreciate that "one cannot NOT communicate." Teacher communication is pervasive and can be unintentional, including nonverbal behaviors that students interpret as communication.
- Watch nonverbal communication. Check out discrepancies perceived in verbal and nonverbal communication with others. Also, audit the nonverbal cues of others whenever there are doubts or questions with regard to meaning, and watch your own body language. Body movements and facial gestures should show a favorable attitude toward students, colleagues, parents, and administrators. They should display a desire to include the other person in communication. Be mindful of the importance of personal space and do not violate the personal space of others. Use an open office or classroom design if you want to facilitate interpersonal communication with students and parents. And, finally, watch time—failure to observe the standards of a school or situation can reduce chances for success in a school organization.
- Don't forget the grapevine. Counter rumors in the grapevine by providing accurate information, challenging the source of a rumor, and encouraging others to recall facts or experiences contrary to the rumor. Be sure to use credible sources of information in communi-

cation—sources students and colleagues will believe. Answer questions directly and specifically whenever possible. Admit uncertainty when it is not possible to do so but explain the causes of the uncertainty.

THREE

Communication and Choice

Mutate your metaphors. — *Karl E. Weick*

Chapters 1 and 2 emphasized that teacher communication involves both command and relational skills. Challenges to effective teacher communication are normal because students are people and people are imprecise, unclear, and unpredictable. This chapter outlines how many of the everyday communication frustrations that teachers experience result from how they perceive communication and its relationship to teaching. Perceptions direct teacher communication behaviors. If teachers assume that meaning is primarily in the words or symbols people use, they see communication as primarily a matter of precision or correct grammar. They can be frustrated with the uncertainties of communication. But if they see meaning as created within people, they can see communication as more than just the definitions of words. Teacher communication is about attitudes, feelings, and emotions. If teachers understand this, they are more prepared to cope with the ambiguities of communication and teaching.

Chapter 3 focuses on *choice* as a fundamental part of teacher communication. Choice is stressed because many teachers assume that circumstances and other people force them to communicate in one way or another. They do not think they have choices when it comes to communication. But teachers always have the choice to respond negatively or thoughtfully to things that happen and to what other people say. The empowering idea of choice can influence a teacher's communication encounters in the future.

29

MUTATING METAPHORS

Developing effective choices in teacher communication means looking at how teachers perceive communication. Teachers who see communication as debate or performance limit communication choices to arguments or stage fright. If teachers are in a "debate," they try to win at communication. Likewise, it is natural for teachers to have stage fright if they feel like they are performing on a stage.

Teachers do not have to see communication as either debate or performance. They can also see communication as *conversation*. Seeing communication as conversation puts communication into a different perspective. People don't have to win conversations or act for the sake of conversational partners. People are less inclined to debate or perform if communication feels more like a conversation and less like a debate or performance.

Karl Weick (1969) explains communication as based on guiding metaphors and uses the phrase *mutate your metaphors* to describe the skill of changing how one sees communication. To Weick, mutating means changing the major images people carry in hearts and minds to describe the communication. He argues that using metaphors often doesn't happen at the conscious level. Effort is required to bring metaphors to awareness. To illustrate this in a Public Speaking for Educators class, I draw a line on the Smart Board that people typically see as a bird or seagull. I ask the class, "What do you see?" They immediately respond, "Bird!" "Seagull!" I ask again, "What do you see?" For a moment, students look confused. But then a hearty soul joins the game and hollers, "Mountains!" Another yells, "A sideways number three?" "Eyebrows!" The responses mount until they reach fifteen or twenty. (I always know when students are fully in the game when someone screams out a part of the human anatomy.) The activity shows that people don't always consciously know how they see things, but perceptions can change if the mind is encouraged to try.

The misuse of metaphors can lead to personal and professional problems. Metaphors are inherently flawed. They are not the things themselves that they represent. They can be misapplied. If a metaphor communicates a narrow, shallow view of an issue or person, it leads to the inability to articulate a workable analysis of a problem and to a careful understanding of a person. For example, if teachers see communication with students as a "war," the metaphor limits thoughtful responses. If teachers expect a war in the classroom, words become "weapons" to attack their "opponents." Teachers are not in the state of mind to let down defenses and to be open to what students have to say or need.

For example, common sports metaphors and other outmoded images—military and consumer—are often overused in education. Educators lose the capacity to think and act appropriately when they are trapped in irrelevant and inappropriate systems of thought and communication. As a communication tool, metaphors are not helpful if rooted in inappropriate comparisons. For example, students are often referred to as "consumers." The metaphor is intended to communicate a sense of entitlement and rights. But it also implies that students are in school to "purchase" an education and not to be engaged. It turns education into a transaction between "buyers" and "sellers." In this case, intellectual challenge may not be the best sales pitch.

Metaphors clarify complex situations by drawing on simpler and more familiar images of life. Teachers' thinking about teaching and students shapes the way they talk and act in the classroom. They can consciously choose when it is useful to see communication one way or another. By mutating metaphors, communication becomes more appropriate for teaching and the classroom.

Choosing How to Communicate

One way for teachers to mutate their communication metaphors and increase their sense of choice is by broadening their view of *interpersonal communication*. As a metaphor, interpersonal communication is limited to what happens between two people—parent and child, teacher and student, principal and teacher—in face-to-face situations. But face-to-face situations are only one way of seeing interpersonal communication. *Interpersonal* can also be a label for a type or quality of communication that can be present in a variety of situations with a variety of people, including in classrooms and with students. Interpersonal communication can happen in various situations—on a smartphone, over the Internet, in texts, in groups, and even in public speaking situations.

Teachers can begin to think of teaching as a possible arena for interpersonal communication. John Stewart (2005)—professor, mentor, and friend—offers the interpersonal-impersonal continuum. It is a visual aid that points to the possibility of integrating interpersonal communication and teaching. The continuum emphasizes that interpersonal communication is not restricted to face-to-face situations but can be a choice that teachers make in all kinds of situations.

Imagine the following continuum:

INTERPERSONAL--IMPERSONAL

This continuum places communication situations on the quality spectrum. It is no longer a question of either impersonal or interpersonal communication but of shades or degrees of each. Teachers move left or right along the continuum depending on the choice to be more or less interpersonal in any particular situation. The continuum raises issues such as: On what does a choice depend? How do teachers know if their communication should be more or less interpersonal? What are the specific qualities at each end of the continuum?

Stewart poses three questions that help teachers make the choice to be more or less interpersonal, all recognizing that communication is situational: (1) Do teachers want to focus on what makes the other person—student, parent, colleague, administrator— unique? (2) Do teachers want to respect the person's ability to think and make choices? Finally,(3) Do teachers want to pay attention to relevant feelings and to the whole human being? Stewart suggests that "yes" should be the response to all three questions about students.

Students are unique and not interchangeable.

An object is the same as any other object in its category. For example, if I want new earphones for a smartphone, any earphones will work, just as any protective case will work to keep a phone shiny and new. Sure, there are differences in quality but the products are basically interchangeable.

Students are never interchangeable. They can be treated that way. One person can replace another person in a task or job, and some students perform better than others and are easier to work with than others. But uniqueness comes from the inside. Individual students see things differently. They have different perspectives. For example, the familiar images of two straight lines (of equal length but with the arrows pointing inward or outward) can be seen either as a candlestick or as a wine glass (or as two faces). The image is an example of how things can be seen differently by different people.

Another example is about witnesses of a traffic accident. There can be very different perspectives on what happened. Each onlooker who witnessed the accident has a slightly different perspective, depending on the view they had, what was going on in their heads, their mood, their powers of observation, and how much danger they felt.

The same principle applies to teaching—each situation, event, and conversation means something different to the students involved. Students give different meanings, according to their belief systems and how they are affected by the interactions. Individual students have their own realities. As Anaïs Nin said, "We don't see things as they are; we see things as we are" (2014).

Students look at situations and interpret them according to their own set of past experiences, culture, faith, and values—their horizons of experience. All of these factors help students formulate beliefs about themselves, about others, and about the world in general. The meanings that students give to events, and the way they make sense of the world, are based on their set of core beliefs and prejudices. They all offer something different. They differ in personal styles and tastes, senses of humor, and future career interests. Although some share similar traits, there is only one of each of them. They are each unique.

Students can think and are capable of making choices.

Avoiding arguments over artificial intelligence, objects don't think like humans. Herbert Dreyfus (1992) argues that objects can only be chosen; they cannot choose. People choose to turn on computers. People choose to initiate actions. A computer seems to operate on its own but is still dependent on choices initiated from the outside. Students are not objects. As constructivist educators David Martin and Kimberly Loomis (2014) argue, students create their own meanings. Teachers may not always like the idea but students initiate their own choices.

This point needs further elaboration. Often "physically challenged" students are treated like objects because they don't appear capable of initiating actions. But there's a difference between the movements of objects and the actions of people. Movements are fundamentally reflexive in nature; actions are reflective. Differently abled students can be limited in movement but are still capable of initiating actions. They are reflective. The issue is not whether physically challenged students can think to act but whether they can communicate those thoughts to initiate actions.

Students have feelings.

This fact distinguishes students from objects more than anything else. For example, if a person kicks a rock, he or she can predict what will happen. With information on force, velocity, momentum, and energy, the person can estimate pretty accurately where the rock will end up after being kicked. At least the rock will not kick back. But try kicking a student (not recommended). What is the student's response? Will the student cry, look surprised, get angry, or kick back? A student's response cannot be as accurately calculated. Brain waves, heart rate, pulse, and respiration can be measured, but that's not the whole story. How students respond emotionally to experiences and events continues to be immeasurable.

Although people are unique, thoughtful, and emotional, teachers need to communicate impersonally sometimes in order to be efficient. In these cases: they focus on general characteristics; they ignore issues of thinking and choice; and they stay away from emotions. For example, when a teacher talks with a kitchen worker in the school lunch line—a situation where there's just two people in a face-to-face encounter (normally what we would think of as an interpersonal situation)—the continuum suggests that communication can be on the impersonal end of the scale. Neither the teacher nor the kitchen worker have the time to hold up a long line of noisy students while they have a personal chat that shows each person's uniqueness, feelings, and choices.

On the other hand, when speaking to an entire class of thirty students in a one-on-many situation, a teacher can be more interpersonal. The continuum simply shows that the difference is in the quality of communication, not in the situation. Even speaking to large groups, teachers can choose to treat people interpersonally by using their names, actively listening to their questions, and respecting their feelings.

It is not that interpersonal communication is always appropriate or that impersonal communication is always inappropriate. Expectations, time constraints, or a multitude of other factors sometimes dictate the only way to deal efficiently with a situation. Although there are no strict rules or formulas for making these communication choices, the continuum offers guidelines to help teachers make effective decisions and emphasizes that it is always our choice to be interpersonal or impersonal in a variety of settings.

TEACHER COMMUNICATION AND PEOPLEMAKING

Interpersonal or relational communication is the source of important information for teachers. It gives teachers a sense of other people's perceptions and emotions. It helps teachers to develop a perspective on problems and issues. In addition, interpersonal communication is a useful approach for teachers who see education as not only the transmission of information but also as the development of character.

For example, relational communication is also about *peoplemaking,* a concept developed by Virginia Satir (1988). Satir defines the quality of each person's life as a result of the quality of his or her communication. Besides being a "tool" to accomplish certain tasks, communication affects who we are and who we become as people. Parents know this. There is a big difference between *what* parents say to a child (the tool part) and *how* they say it (the peoplemaking part). Parents can say "I love you" in two very different ways—one way tells the child to be reassured that he or she is worthy of love; the other way can be said with sarcasm and conflicting nonverbal messages (the double bind), confusing the child and manipulating his or her emotions.

The peoplemaking metaphor is useful for thinking about the kind of people teachers want to help "make." Communicative understanding is never the result of one person. People never communicate in a vacuum. Even when reading a book, more than one individual is involved. Communication and understanding emerge within human interaction. Teacher interaction helps make students the people they are and will become. Whenever teachers communicate, they "fuse" horizons with a student. They help make new people with new understandings, whether positive or negative. The peoplemaking metaphor highlights the central connection of teacher communication and human relations. It suggests that teachers and their communication play a profound role in helping students to become productive and healthy human beings.

CLASSROOM COMMUNICATION CLIMATES

Teacher communication affects students and the kind of people they become. Moving beyond individuals, one question is whether the same principles apply to the classroom or learning climate. If teachers are concerned about the kind of people communication creates, they also need to be concerned about the kind of people classroom communication creates.

Once again, Charles Conrad helps us understand a connection between classroom communication climate, student attitudes, and student achievement. Conrad establishes that productivity (what teachers call *student achievement*) and job satisfaction (what teachers call *student attitudes*) are related. He points to studies conducted between 1927 and 1932 at the Hawthorne Plant of the Western Electric Company in Cicero, Illinois, that showed that employees who worked in friendly, relaxed, and congenial atmospheres with concerned and supportive supervisors were more productive and satisfied than workers in not so favorable conditions. The results of the studies, known as the Hawthorne effect, can apply to teachers and students. As one way of seeing teachers and students, they can be likened to supervisors and employees (Meir, 2009).

For example, Colby Pearce (2012) assessed fourteen children who were of concern to a staff member at the school hosting the study. The children were assessed in terms of their engagement and behavior. Pearce's assessment included interviews of each child, their parent(s), their classroom teacher, and administrators at the school. He prepared a diagnostic report for each child and made recommendations regarding each child's care and management requirements. He also conducted individual feedback sessions with the parents of each child, and with their teacher, and provided general training to staff of the school about engaging children who are disengaged and who exhibit challenging behavior in school. Pearce returned to the school approximately six months later.

The results of Pearce's assessments and interventions showed that only one of the original fourteen children continued to be of concern to school authorities in terms of their engagement and behavior. Pearce showed that student satisfaction with social and interpersonal relationships with peers and teachers significantly influenced engagement and behavior. In other words, he found that the Hawthorne effect applies to the classroom setting. Classroom communication climates affect the engagement and behavior of students.

In addition, McCroskey and colleagues (1996) found that increased learning is related to teacher immediacy—approachability, understanding, friendliness, imagination, learner-centeredness, positive attitudes toward students, and democratic practices. Darling and Civikly (1987) also found that a supportive classroom communication climate results in more student achievement. Positive teacher communication improves student attitudes and learning performance.

The studies suggest that there are things teachers can do to contribute to positive peoplemaking and increased student satisfaction and learning, including the following:

- Recognize students' uniqueness by carefully assigning tasks that fit the characteristics and skills of the learner. An effective way for teachers to view student satisfaction and learning is as outcomes of student-centered learning, what Jennifer Waldeck (2007) calls *personalized education*.Teachers should attempt to know their students, to be accessible, to adjust curriculum to individual student needs, and to communicate in a warm, friendly manner. Scott Myers and Alan Goodboy (2009) agree that learning is increased when students see the classroom as personalized and see teacher communication as supportive, confirming, and immediate.
- Appreciate that students are thinkers and give them responsibilities complex enough to challenge them but simple enough to accomplish. An assignment or project that is too complex is frustrating and not satisfying to students. When assignments are too simple, they become boring. When too complex, they become disheartening. Effective challenges require a balance.
- Develop the "whole" student by establishing a positive classroom communication climate. A classroom communication climate is a frame of reference for shaping student expectations, attitudes, feelings, and behaviors. It influences learning outcomes.

Teacher communication practices sustain student satisfaction and learning by helping create positive classroom communication climates. Classroom communication climates are strongly mediated by teacher communication practices. Ellis Hays (1970) recognizes that teacher communication helps students develop impressions of a classroom as being either supportive or defensive environments. Impressions of supportive climates result from teachers being straightforward and honest, treating students as equals, and helping students to feel understood. Impressions of defensive climates result from teachers treating some students as favorites, being psychologically manipulative, and expressing dogmatic opinions.

One outcome of supportive teacher practices is a student's sense of classroom connectedness, or the perception of cooperation, support, and community in a classroom. Dwyer and colleagues (2004) found that teacher communication behaviors that encourage classroom respect, dignity, a sense of community, and a lack of judgmental opinions also encourage a connected classroom. When students feel connected, they feel rapport with their teacher and classmates. W. Charles Redding (1972) identifies five major components of effective connectedness and community. Redding's components suggest the crucial role of superior–subordinate or teacher–student communication. The components include the degree to which a teacher:

- Is *supportive* of students' efforts.
- Permits *participative decision making*.
- Has the *trust* of students.
- Encourages *open communication*.
- Communicates *high expectations*.

In addition, Frederick Jablin (1979) adds a couple items to the list:

- Power—students who perceive teachers as using power and authority justly communicate more frequently with them.
- Information gap—too wide a gap between teacher and students makes communication less effective; too thin a gap decreases diversity of information and interpretations of issues.

CONCLUSION

As this chapter outlined, teacher communication involves how teachers perceive communication and teacher–student relationships. Changing guiding metaphors helps to reveal different communication choices to teachers. An impersonal classroom setting can be reframed to have interpersonal possibilities. An interaction with a student typically seen only as a phase of task completion can become an opportunity to influence the quality of the student's life and character.

Overall, the previous two chapters reinforced that effective teacher communication is two-fold. It encompasses the ability to transmit clear and accurate commands and the ability to maintain positive relationships with students. In fact, this chapter tilted the balance between these two functions to the relational side. It agrees with the German philosopher Karl Jaspers (1960) that our "supreme achievement in the world is communication from personality to personality."

The next chapter introduces a model for developing teacher communication competence. As a preview, here are four suggestions for establishing a foundation for such competence:

- Watch your communication metaphors. Effective communication in today's classrooms begins with more productive and positive images of students and teacher communication.

- Build choice into your communication behaviors. Teachers decide how to communicate through past choices, perceptions of the current situation, and the ability to see communication situations differently. By assuming they have communication choices, teachers can generate creative possibilities.
- Choose to be interpersonal in appropriate situations. Teachers can look for opportunities to treat students and colleagues as unique, feeling, and thinking human beings. By acknowledging that even a simple hello in the hallway helps build connectedness, teachers can build positive student relationships.
- Actively contribute to a positive classroom communication climate. When appropriate, teachers can use supportive communication to encourage democratic decision-making and to build collective trust in the classroom. Practice open communication and set high but reasonable standards.

FOUR

Teacher Communication Competence

> If you want to truly understand something, try to change it.
> —*Kurt Lewin*

Chapter 3 showed how everyday teacher communication is influenced by teacher perceptions about communication and relationships. Choice is a necessary part of effective teacher communication. Teachers always have a choice in communication to respond either negatively or positively to students and others and to be either interpersonal or impersonal. Teacher perceptions of communication affect their ability to make effective choices.

This chapter moves beyond perception and concentrates on a practical approach for developing teacher communication competence. Effective teaching depends to a great extent on the communication knowledge and performance of the teacher. Teachers perform many roles and functions in the teaching and learning process. Whether addressing students, parents, administrators, or counselors, teachers need to be competent communicators.

Specifically, chapter 4 identifies a set of communication competencies that synthesize issues already raised in this book and aligns those issues with specific communication recommendations from the Secretary of Labor's Commission on Achieving Necessary Skills (SCANS) in the workplace (1991). The objective is to show what thinking and communication skills are necessary for effective teaching in the contemporary classroom where the advent of high-stakes testing and new technologies challenge the importance of relational communication.

Following a discussion of SCANS, the chapter presents an integrative model of teacher communication competence that offers a practical approach for enhancing communication skills and for balancing thought and action. The model assumes that it is not enough for teachers to know their communication options; they must also reflect about and "try on" the behaviors in real situations. The model offers workable guidelines for developing teacher communication competence.

THE DEMANDS OF TEACHER COMMUNICATION

So far, this book has concentrated on teacher communication functions and the importance of choice in teacher communication behaviors. It is time to show how those issues can be translated into the skills teachers need to improve communication in the classroom and school. To begin, SCANS was asked originally to examine the level of communication skills required to succeed in the workplace. In carrying out this charge, the commission identified communication skills also needed for the teaching profession.

The commission agreed that workplace know-how is essentially made up of command and relational communication skills as discussed in previous chapters. It observed that know-how has two main elements: competencies (knowledge) and foundations (skills). The report identifies three competencies already discussed in this book that directly relate to teacher communication: information competency (command), interpersonal competency (relational), and systems competency (climate).

Information competency is the knowledge and skills teachers need to acquire and use information, or what this book refers to as *command communication*. It includes four major attributes. Teachers must do the following:

- Acquire and evaluate information.
- Organize and maintain information.
- Interpret and communicate information.
- Use information technology to process information.

Interpersonal competency is the knowledge and skills teachers need to work with others, or what this book refers to as *relational communication*. It emphasizes six areas of relational communication. Teachers must do the following:

- Participate in teams and contribute to effective group communication.
- Communicate knowledge and skills to others.
- Communicate to satisfy product (outcomes) and process (methods) expectations.
- Communicate to persuade others about challenges, procedures, and policies.
- Negotiate with others through divergent interests toward agreements.
- Communicate well with people from diverse backgrounds.

Systems competency is the knowledge and skill teachers need to understand complex social and organizational interrelationships, or what this book refers to as *communication climates*. It stresses the dynamic of systematic change and development that exists among teachers and students in the contemporary classroom. Teachers must do the following:

- Know how social, organizational, and technological systems function effectively in the classroom.
- Evaluate trends and impacts on classroom operations and dynamics.
- Develop new and alternative systems to improve student performance and learning in future classrooms.

The SCANS competencies are an organizing device for making sense of teacher communication and for putting information presented in this book into practice. They lead the way for developing teacher communication competence. In the next section, the book offers a model for teachers to assess their own communication proficiency and to plan their own communication development.

TEACHER COMMUNICATION COMPETENCE MODEL

To reflect the SCANS competencies, teachers can look to a model for developing teacher communication competence based on the works of Rebecca Rubin and Jerry Feezel (1986), and R. R. Allen and Kenneth L. Brown (1976). Collectively, they contribute a four-stage model of teacher communication competence that helps teachers assess their SCANS competencies through ordinary skills of watching, choosing, doing and reflecting.

Many workshops, experiences, and courses for developing teacher communication competence skills focus on supplying "rules" that treat communication behavior as a logical equation, a sort of "If/Then" procedure. The role of communication choice and relational communication is ignored. The teacher communication competence model below is different. It does not present ideas in terms of rules. It trains teachers to think in terms of guidelines for communication behavior. Guidelines leave room for individual reflection and choice. No two communication situations are ever alike, so no one rule will always work.

To be competent communicators, teachers must have continuing experiences from which to learn and reflect on their own actions. To be more competent communicators, teachers can focus on developing, choosing, practicing, and evaluating a repertoire of communication skills.

Develop a Repertoire of Communication Skills

Teachers must be flexible actors, capable of performing a wide range of communication acts as required by the students, settings, and tasks of the classroom. The first element of teacher communication competence is building a knowledge base by observing the communication performance of others. By watching others, teachers build a list, or *repertoire*, of available communication acts. Some call this a "bag of tricks" or "toolbox" of teacher communication skills.

Choose Appropriate Communication Skills

Teacher communication competence is also based on the *appropriateness* of behaviors in particular educational situations; consideration toward other people, time, place, and subject matter; and a teacher's goal or purpose. Competent communicators understand that specific communication skills do not work in all situations or for all people, and they choose appropriate communication. They make judgments about circumstances and determine the correct communication skill needed.

For example, when in college, I admired a history professor. One of his communication behaviors was to lecture word-for-word from a prepared manuscript. When I began teaching my own history class, I tried speaking word-for-word from a manuscript. It was a disaster! I realized that my lecture style is more conversational. I like wiggle room to think about a subject as I lecture and to change it depending on questions and responses from my students. My history professor's skills were not appropriate for me. I had to make my own judgment about the correct communication skill for my needs.

Practice Communication Skills

After teachers choose a communication act that is appropriate for a particular situation, they must *"try on"* the behavior. They must perform the act and demonstrate the ability to act on their choice. They must apply a communication behavior. Of course, it is best that they first practice in a "safe" situation. For example, in communication courses or training sessions, teachers get to practice communication behaviors in supportive learning environments. Everyone in a communication course or workshop is in the same boat. Each person needs the support of others to keep his or her head above water. Participants learn very quickly to offer encouragement and constructive criticism if they want to receive the same.

Evaluate Communication Skills

Teachers cannot depend on rules to communicate effectively but must reflect on their own communication behavior and *evaluate* it in terms of satisfaction. Competent communicators do not beat themselves up. Their internal dialogue, or self-talk, does not say such things as, "I'm a failure," or "I'm terrible!" Instead, competent communicators ask themselves, "What can I do better next time?" They exhibit a growth mindset. They see themselves as capable learners and look toward a positive future.

CHARACTERISTICS OF COMMUNICATION COMPETENCE

The teacher communication competence model consists of four major components:

- Knowledge — building a repertoire of communication skills
- Judgment — choosing appropriate communication skills
- Practice — trying new communication skills
- Evaluation — reflecting and assessing satisfaction with communication skills

Based on the assumption that the above components require dynamic learning experiences and individual reflection, teacher communication competence can also be described by four important characteristics: it is *situational, thoughtful, functional, and purposeful.*

Competence Is Situational

A teacher does not simply possess communication competence. Rather, competence is always a matter of degree depending on the situation. A teacher is never entirely competent or incompetent as a communicator but is more or less so. Teachers vary in levels of communication competence from moment to moment and from situation to situation. Competent communicators are always learning. They learn by observing the communication behaviors of other teachers and by trying on behaviors themselves. Teacher communication competence requires openness to learning and willingness to risk trying new skills.

Someone highly competent in one situation may be incompetent in a different situation. Thomas Paine was extremely competent at communicating the need for the American Revolution but incompetent at communicating the specific details of a new government. The latter bored him. The lesson of Thomas Paine for teachers is that flexibility and adaptability are associated with communication competence. Teachers need to know their communication strengths and weaknesses. Then they can reflect on what areas need improvement.

Competence Is Thoughtful

Teacher communication competence is not in and of itself a trait that teachers possess but is the recognition of strengths and weaknesses, and the appropriateness of a specific communication act to a specific situation. It requires discerning and thinking. It needs the judgment of a teacher. For example, a competent teacher understands that aggressive defense of a teacher's ideas may not be appropriate in a classroom of respectful learners but is perfectly appropriate in another setting. Attacking another person's ideas in a brainstorming session is not appropriate, but it's appropriate to help create a safe environment that permits people to take intellectual risks. Teacher communication competence is largely a function of the analysis of particular situations and what communication skills are appropriate. Consequently, it requires experience and reflection.

Competence Is Functional

Teacher competence means accomplishing things by communicating (commands) and maintaining productive relationships (relational). Teachers must meet both goals with their communication for it to be valuable for themselves or others. Competent communicators need to translate knowledge into skills. Knowledge involves the sense of how to communicate in an appropriate way, and skill is the ability to actually do so. Competent communication is a balancing act. Teachers need to balance command with relational communication, and they must balance communication theory with action. In fact, balance is what it means to function competently.

Competence Is Purposeful

An important criterion of teacher communication competence is satisfaction with an outcome. How satisfying are the results of a communication behavior for a teacher? Did the outcome of the communication act satisfy the goal? Did it work well in terms of a particular objective? The purpose of a communication act needs to be an important element in whether a teacher judges the act to be satisfactory. Satisfaction with a communication act is always a function of its purpose. The process should lead to a satisfying product. How satisfactory communication interaction is judged depends largely on what was expected.

Whether a teacher is writing an email, chatting with a member of a team, or giving a presentation, he or she has a communication purpose. Competent communicators know the purpose of communication. Teachers should ask themselves a number of questions about their communication purpose:

- What is the main, overriding purpose?
- Is there anything that needs to be changed?
- Is the communication purpose to move people to act?
- Is there anything the audience should do after the communication?

A COMMUNICATION COMPETENCE PLAN

Teachers need to understand the elements and characteristics of competent communication and how to plan for change. They must understand the means for improving communication skills. This next section provides specific ways for developing teacher communication competence.

Kurt Lewin (1946) described change as a three-step process, requiring teachers to (1) "unfreeze" old communication behaviors through reflection and training; (2) "move" toward new communication behaviors by trying on new behaviors; and (3) "refreeze" new communication behaviors through reaching satisfaction and self-support. The following items help teachers to unfreeze old communication behaviors and plan for improved communication skills. They are all forms of training and serve as catalysts for transforming one's self into a person willing to try new behaviors. By incorporating these ideas into daily routines, teachers can become intentional change agents and can refreeze a new set of teacher communication skills.

Teachers who want to intentionally plan a process for communication improvement and for developing teacher communication competence can incorporate the following activities into their repertoire.

Elicit Feedback from Others

A basic strategy for developing teacher communication competence, and a great source of professional growth, is gathering feedback. Teachers get feedback from as many different interactions as possible. There is no better way to learn about communication performance than to review how things went. For example, groups or teams can donate time at the end of every session to how the team process went. Five minutes of discussion at the end of a meeting about the strengths and weaknesses of the group process contributes to the group effort, helps organize and maintain information, and can modify the process in order to improve team performance. Classes can also spend time at the end of a discussion talking about what elements of the discussion worked well and what the class wants to do differently next time. Even teachers can ask students at the end of an activity what seemed to work and what needs improvement. Most students are willing to give meaningful feedback if they think the information will be used to improve teaching and learning.

Get a Mentor

Another great source of support and stimulus to a teacher's professional growth is to team up with a colleague as either a peer or an apprentice. Dr. Lois J. Zachary (2011) observes that a mentoring relationship means sharing, testing, modifying, defending, and articulating values, concepts, rationales, designs, and techniques. It is an opportunity to observe the communication performance of another teacher, elicit feedback in a safe environment, debrief each other, and learn from shared experience. Observing a teacher's classroom or allowing another teacher to visit your classroom is an excellent way to get valuable feedback.

Part of service to my college is being available as a mentor to colleagues by facilitating a method called the Small Group Instructional Diagnosis (SGID) for colleagues interested in finding out how their teaching is going. The process is anonymous and confidential for both the instructor and the students. It involves going into the classroom without the teacher and breaking students into groups of four to five. The students are asked these questions: "What helps you learn in this class?" and "What improvements need to be done and how would you make them?" Groups have five minutes each to respond to the questions. Groups share responses with the whole class to identify disagreements and to reach some level of consensus. Both teachers and students appreciate the method. Teachers get specific ideas about how to improve teaching, and students get to see the results of their feedback put into action in the class. As the facilitator, I also get mentored. I learn more from the procedure than the teachers who request it.

Document Communication Events

To improve communication, teachers must keep a record of their communication behaviors. They must document what they do and see as communicators. Documentation is a means for collecting the list of communication responses for a repertoire of knowledge and skills. Logs, journals, and diaries are effective tools for recording observations and judgments. They help teachers identify new communication skills and are excellent tools for reflection. Self-documentation is the basis of setting communication goals. A teacher needs clear targets for improving communication competence. A number of communication inventories and self-help materials provide direction and activities for teachers to engage systematically in communication improvement.

Participate in Professional Development

Some of the most interesting and supportive professional opportunities for developing teacher communication competence come from being an active member in a professional association. It helps to be affiliated with one or more such groups and to participate in their activities. Being a member offers opportunities for communicating in teams and for exercising leadership. Presenting a workshop at a professional conference is an excellent way to learn.

Share Experiences with Others

Many teachers are inhibited about asking other teachers what they do and how they do it. However, curiosity reflects a desire to learn that can be very rewarding. The exchange of concrete stories about communication successes and failures is probably the most useful resource for developing teacher communication competence.

Take Risks

Improving communication requires a willingness to risk new learning opportunities. Taking a communication course or workshop is risky. Going back to school is not easy. There are concerns about money, work obligations, and family responsibilities. School and tests can challenge self-esteem, require tight schedules, and increase responsibilities. But taking risks is a source of growth, stimulation, knowledge, and skills. It gives teachers experience with people from diverse backgrounds who are also interested in learning.

Read

It is essential to develop a reading program to improve teacher communication competence. This includes college texts, articles, research papers, journals, papers, and magazines. Reading journals like *Communication Education* is an excellent idea. The challenge, of course, is to develop the self-discipline to set aside time for reading. But the reading program has already begun. Reading this book starts the process of developing teacher communication competence. The next challenge is to find ways to apply the information and go beyond the confines of ideas alone.

CONCLUSION

The development of teacher communication competence happens in many ways. It can happen through formal schooling with readings and assignments, including deadlines, or it can happen through informal means and within the venue of personal activities. Whatever the nature of the experience, a plan is an important part of the process. The major difference between the desire to improve teacher communication and its realization is a blueprint for what is needed and how to proceed.

This chapter offered a blueprint. The teacher communication competence model provides a way for making sense of communication experiences and for enhancing teacher communication skills. It does not depend on rules but on the ability of teachers to observe communication
behaviors and to reflect on those actions. Following are a few final suggestions for using the model to get the most out of the remainder of this
book.

Develop a Repertoire of Teacher Communication Skills

Reading this book should not be a passive process. Reading is an
active and selective process. To learn how to become a competent communicator, teachers must actively identify and select the skills they need.

Choose Appropriate Communication Skills for a Situation

An active learner in all aspects of understanding pays attention to the
information that is most relevant to his or her own needs. Learning to be
a competent teacher communicator is about applying your ideas for your
own purposes. Application can begin with reading and reflecting on how
the ideas in this book apply to personal teaching and relationships.

Try on New Communication Behaviors in Safe Situations

After selecting appropriate skills, decide how to "try on" the behaviors. When teachers are exposed to the skills taught in this book, they
often attempt to try them out in difficult situations. They may try effective listening skills in interactions that are most likely to trigger judgments. They might be assertive with the persons least likely to respond to
such messages. Just as it is foolhardy to enter a marathon without first
training to run, it is unwise to try new communication skills in challenging situations before trying them in safer settings.

Try a Specific Skill Weekly

The decision to try a specific communication skill each week is an
important commitment. Unless committed to a specific skill each week, it
is easy to think that skills are being more utilized than they are. Remember, teacher communication competence is not just knowing skills but
also trying them.

Reflect on Communication Behavior

Learn to apply "retrospective sense-making" to teacher communication acts. Pay attention to how satisfying communication behaviors are.
After an encounter, learn to ask people such questions as, "How do you

think that went?" Or ask students, "Is that clear?" Interpret responses as statements about your own communication. Continue to identify communication strengths and areas for improvement. Finally, be open to learning and seeing teaching as a way of communicating.

II

Teaching and Organizational Communication

> Communication networks in organizations are analogous to the nervous system within the human body. — *Susan A. Hellweg*

You could say this book's theme is "Communication abounds in all areas of teaching" a topic currently inspiring educational researchers to study social and relational networks in school organizations. Gerald Goldhaber (1990) defines an organization as social networks of interdependent relationships. As members of networks, teachers are interdependent; they affect and are affected by one another. In any school, communication travels and connects through a multitude of networks. Through everyday communication, teachers and administrators interact and relate.

Social networks provide structure and stability to schools. Networks are the means by which school messages flow, information is disseminated, tasks are coordinated, and decisions are made. Social networks help organizational conflicts to be resolved and staff performance to be appraised. They define communication channels and permit a school to achieve some level of predictability.

The organizational patterns of school information and communication are determined formally by the distribution of resources and assigned positions, and informally by the immediate needs and communication networks of school members. Teachers work in various networks for different organizational functions, some involving formal and informal relationships. Teachers become members of social networks as a function of organizational responsibilities, issues, or socialization.

Today's primary and secondary schools have the additional communication factor of electronic social networks such as email, Facebook, and Twitter. A fully technologically networked school offers several benefits for teachers by allowing them to do the following:

- Share files faster and more reliably than traditional networks. Central printers can be made accessible more conveniently.

- Carry out everyday communications with each other more efficiently. News and class project information can be easily disseminated to students.
- Collaborate more easily on group projects using network software applications.

This section looks at the topic of school networks. First, it looks at the organizational structure of social networks in school. Second, it discusses the functions of social networks such as centralization, decentralization, roles, and links. Finally, it introduces effective learning relationships as a crucial element for productive teacher relationships, communication, and networks in school participation.

THE SOCIAL NETWORKS OF SCHOOLS

A social network is a repetitive pattern of information exchange among groups in school organizations. Perhaps the most commonly understood network is the formal organizational chart. Organizational charts are made up of official positional relationships defined by the authority and functional duties of teachers, administrators, and staff. They represent the organizational hierarchy of reporting relationships. They dictate who communicates to whom formally and establish the school's organizational structure.

Many researchers of school organization agree that the emphasis on formal positions and relationships have two main advantages:

- Tasks get accomplished more efficiently, and
- Conflict resulting from different people doing the same thing is reduced.

From a teacher's perspective, formal positions clarify the nature of relationships and reduce the amount of friction, insecurity, and inefficiency that can result from uncertain and ambiguous relationships. The most common formal relationship in school organizations is the *teacher–administrator relationship*. Administrators and teachers communicate on a frequent basis as a function of their formal relationships. The communication and working relationship between an administrator, such as a principal, and teachers is a crucial dynamic for the efficient and effective functioning of schools. On the other hand, formal positional relationships can also hamper a school's efficiency and effectiveness. Teachers often tell principals what they think the administrator wants to hear, or what the teacher wants the administrator to hear—information that reflects favorably on the teacher. Consequently, the quality of teacher–administrator communication can have negative consequences for a school by failing to address poor teacher performance or reinforcing poor administrative policies.

Moolennar and colleagues (2012) find that informal social networks are also intertwined within a school organization and provide a major function for the school. They create an organizational structure all their own. While formal networks serve as a blueprint for how teachers are supposed to communicate, informal networks often reflect how they actually do communicate. They translate messages carried over formal networks and move those messages forward faster than in formal channels. On the other hand, informal social networks can also contribute to a school's inefficiency and ineffectiveness through faulty and incomplete information. Informal networks are prone to selective distortion whereby members highlight some information from formal communication and forget about other information.

Social networks are synonymous with organizational transactions. Teachers exchange information and responsibilities for favorable outcomes in decision-making or problem-solving. The principle of transaction is built on the "give a little, get a little" idea of human interaction. *Giving* contributes to organizational processes and participation. *Getting* is what teachers gain for making contributions.

Social networks are the articulation of school transactions and reveal what exchanges are being made. The goals of one group usually require the cooperation of other groups. Transactions among group members give rise to participation based on command and relational communication—what and how people respond to each other. Participation in school social networks help teachers to

- Maximize their goals and
- Develop a system for equitably distributing resources among school members.

Social Network Structures

A social network is a pattern of communicative interaction within a group. Communicating—listening, making statements, asking questions, providing summaries, and leading discussions—is how teachers relate in groups. Organizational researchers Harold Leavitt (1951) and Fred C. Lunenberg (2011) identify different structures or patterns of social networks (see figure 4.1) depending on the level of centralization or who has formal or informal authority. Three networks are classified as centralized social networks. For example, the central person in a *wheel network* is usually the leader and benefits from the position more than those on the periphery whose communication is much more limited. The wheel network is the most structured and centralized of the patterns because each member can communicate with only one other person at a time. A superintendent of schools and his or her immediate subordinates (assistant superintendents) often form a wheel network. The superintendent is the central position, and assistant superintendents are the corner positions. The four assistants send information to the superintendent and the superintendent sends that information back to them, usually in the form of decisions. The wheel network results in faster decision-making and group morale.

The *chain* is the second highest centralized social network. Only two people communicate with one another, and they in turn communicate with one person. Information is sent through a chain network in relay fashion. A typical chain network is one in which a teacher (at the bottom of the chain) reports to the department head, who reports to the principal, who reports to the superintendent (at the top). The chain network results in better control of information flow but is strictly hierarchical. It allows only for vertical movement.

The *Y network* is similar to the chain except that two members fall outside the chain. In the Y network, members in the outside positions or nodes send information to the central node, but they only receive information from that central position. The central position exchanges information with all three of the other positions. For example, two teachers (upper two nodes of the Y network) report to the principal (central position). The principal then reports to the superintendent (lower single node). The Y network is less centralized than the wheel but more centralized than many other patterns.

Social networks like the wheel are centralized and encourage dependency on a leader. Wheel networks can also result in lower group satisfaction. Likewise, the chain and Y school networks limit members to communicating with one or two other people but not with all others in

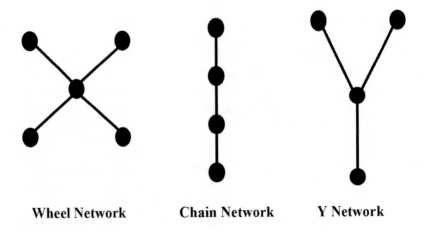

Wheel Network   **Chain Network**   **Y Network**

Figure 4.1. Centralized Social Networks.

the group. The downside of centralization is that it decreases satisfaction and allows for relatively fewer information transactions.

Researchers also identify two decentralized social networks (see figure 4.2). The *circle network* is very different from centralized networks. It represents horizontal and relational communication by giving every member equal communication opportunities. Each member communicates with persons to the right and left. Members have identical limitations, and the circle is less restricting than in centralized networks. In the circle network, everyone has the same authority or power to influence the group. The main problem is that information moves rather slowly and it's more difficult to reach consensus. But morale is high because everyone takes part in decision making.

The *all-channel network* is an extension of the circle network. By relating everyone in the circle network, the result is an all-channel network. The all-channel network permits each teacher to communicate freely with all other teachers in the network. This network has no central position, and no communication restrictions are placed on any member. A committee in which no member either formally or informally assumes a leadership position is a good example of an all-channel network. It is often referred to as the most democratic form of social network.

Social Network Roles

A social network consists of two fundamental parts: *functional* roles and *relational links*.

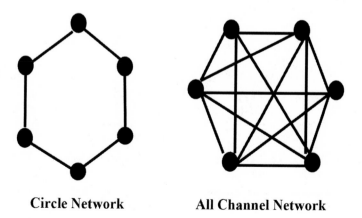

Circle Network   **All Channel Network**

Figure 4.2. Decentralized Social Networks

Functional roles

Members play functional roles as a result of positions and network structures. *Functional roles* can be seen as command (task) and relational (process) oriented. Functional group roles are directed toward both accomplishing the group's task through systematic problem-solving and helping the interpersonal process of the group.

Examples of functional group roles include the following:

- Gatekeepers—Praise, agree with, and accept the ideas of others in the group. They encourage the participation of others, especially placators (see below).
- Harmonizers—Mediate group conflicts and relieve tension, often through appropriate humor. They attempt to create a safe environment for people to participate and contribute. They attempt especially to harmonize pouncers (see below).
- Standard setters—Raise questions of goals and purpose, express standards for the group, and assess movement toward goals. They are an effective counter to the distractor (see below).
- Humanizers—Show an interest in the process or human relations aspect of group work. They are process-oriented and offer some balance to computers (see below). They encourage some discussion of feelings.

Some examples of dysfunctional group roles are offered by Virginia Satir (1988) and are important to teachers managing relationships in group work or facilitating student group work in the classroom. They include the following:

- Placators—Isolate themselves from other group members and turn over decisions to those members. Placators treat the communication system as closed to them by withholding input and denying their own point of view. They may be less secure in their self-concepts or less motivated to accomplish tasks. They can also serve as friendly followers and go along passively.
- Pouncers—Dominate a discussion or decision and tell other group members what they should be doing, how to do it, and who should do it. They tend to intimidate other group members, especially placators, into submission. They like to give orders and to force others to agree with them. They also deflate and antagonize others.
- Distractors—Keep the group off the subject or task. They may "nitpick" by dwelling on unimportant issues and nonessential considerations like the meaning of words or use the group to get personal attention or sympathy. Distractors direct groups away from goals and toward individual concerns.
- Computers—Show no interest in the process or human relations aspect of group work. They are extremely task-oriented. They may

not want to dominate the group and show no inclination to force opinions, but they desire to finish the task even at the expense of another's input, feelings, and social interaction. They lead a group to make decisions not shared by all members and guarantee poor performance.

Relational Links

Teachers often serve as *relational links* between social networks. For example, liaisons act as links between two or more school networks without necessarily belonging to either one of them. As liaisons, teachers coordinate the activities of the networks exchanging information. They are the initial source of information and are highly influential because they have significant control over information flow. An example of a liaison is a department head who carries messages between a principal and teachers under the liaison's supervision.

Links are characterized by five properties:

- Symmetry — the degree to which the members connect by a link and relate on an equity basis.
- Strength — the frequency of interaction among members.
- Reciprocity — the extent to which members agree within their relational links.
- Content — the informational focus of the interaction.
- Mode — the channel or means of communicating.

If teachers give and take information relatively equally, the relationship is symmetrical. If they communicate often, it is considered strong. If teachers believe they agree often with one another, the link is reciprocal. The content of links can be about work, social matters, or other subjects. Information can be communicated in various modes: face-to-face, through meetings, by telephone, or via computer.

This section has outlined some key concepts and issues related to the social network aspect of teacher communication skills. The following section concludes with an introduction to effective learning relationships.

CONCLUSION

An important feature of social network theory is the social relationships that link individual members. Teachers, students, parents, and administrators develop relational ties that knit the social fabric of the school. Effective relationships strengthen communication and clarify interpersonal boundaries. Effective relationships help teachers support themselves, students, parents, and colleagues in the achievement of educational objectives.

Effective learning relationships are interpersonal, communal, and dialogical in nature. Chapter 3 defined interpersonal communication as a quality of communication that emphasizes the uniqueness, choices, and feelings of another person. It is the interpersonal, communal, and dialogical nature of teacher communication and relationships that apply directly to the following chapters in this section. In effective learning relationships, no one is excluded. There is a sense of mutual sharing where participants define and assert their own identities and interests, giving and getting information, and generally participating in social interaction. A sense of belonging is central to the process.

Chapter 5 explains the concept of effective learning relationships—where teachers and students perceive a balance in the amount and quality of communication. The experience is quite different than in more traditional teacher-centered approaches. Understanding and learning become, as Hans-Georg Gadamer (1989) observes, an experience in "participating immediately in life" (p. 211). Education becomes bigger than simply a teacher and a learner. In fact, learning is the goal and outcome for all participants.

Effective learning relationships provide a major communication guideline for teachers: *Interpersonal relationships exert a powerful and pervasive influence over learning.* Kim Worth (2014) recognizes that when teachers build effective learning relationships with students, they help create conditions for good interpersonal relationships and students repond positively with a willingness to share in the learning experience. The purpose of chapters 6 and 7 is to help teachers see how communication helps create effective learning relationships with parents and administrators. Chapter 8 concludes the section with a discussion about communication and conflict. It shows how dealing productively with conflict promotes effective learning relationships.

FIVE

Effective Learning Relationships

> Improving students' relationships with teachers has important, positive and long-lasting implications for both student academic and social development. — *Sara Rimm-Kaufman and Lia Sandilos*

This chapter describes major characteristics of effective learning relationships—most importantly, Étienne Wenger's (1998) *communities of practice* and Hans-George Gadamer's (1989) concept of *dialogue*. Both concepts move further away from the command- and message-oriented model of teacher communication described in chapter 1 and to a more transformational and peoplemaking model introduced in chapter 2. An effective learning relationship and its main elements—communities of practice and dialogue—include factors that have considerable influence on the quality and tone of teacher communication. The elements suggest specific attitudes and skills that teachers may wish to possess.

EFFECTIVE LEARNING RELATIONSHIPS

As observed earlier, effective teacher communication and learning relationships go hand-in-hand—they are inseparable. An effective learning relationship is one where interaction helps teachers and students learn about a subject matter or task, about themselves, and about relating to others. Learning about content, self-identity, and others is enabled within communication. Mutual communication is the air that effective learning relationships breathe.

Relationships without reciprocal communication and interaction do not make for good teaching or learning—they are not effective. Effective learning relationships require communication practices that encourage an interdependent classroom climate, a sense of community, mutual relationships, and student involvement. They create experiences of sharing and belonging where both teacher and student learn content and construct their own identities. They are practices of authentic social participation.

Étienne Wenger argues that authentic social participation and identity construction are essential to experiencing effective learning relationships. For Wenger, learning is a matter of interpersonal and intrapersonal competence in a valued collective endeavor or project. Through social participation and self-identification, learning is sharing ways of engaging and doing things together. Participating in a community is central to Wenger's description. Effective learning relationships happen in what he calls *communities of practice*—where learners experience a sense of belonging to a "commonwealth" through the actions of exploration, engagement, and connection with others. Similar to C. S. Pierce's communities of inquiry and John Dewey's principle of learning through occupation, communities of practice help learners develop a sense of belonging and negotiate meaning with fellow learners. To Wenger, the acquisition of skills and information is secondary. Foremost is the construction of identities and modes of belonging.

Wenger looks to sustained mutual relationships to facilitate shared ways of engaging information and doing things together. His view on education involves more relational than traditional approaches to teaching and learning. Teaching becomes a process of designing tasks that are personally meaningful to students. Education is not primarily teaching techniques to deliver curriculum and transmit knowledge but happens in a particular type of learning environment—a way of organizing and relating—where students construct meaning and form identities together.

In other words, Wenger's approach emphasizes knowledge learning and peoplemaking concurrently, providing teachers with a rationale and general vision for structuring effective learning relationships. The uniqueness of the approach is not necessarily in the information and techniques taught but in the learning environment created. Because of the need to participate in a valued enterprise, students are motivated to share ways of communicating and do communication together. Their participation, interaction, and sense of belonging to a community are central. Identification comes first; information and techniques follow.

In the next section, I describe another conceptual framework that bridges Wenger's theory with more specific instructional practices.

Relationships and Dialogue

It is challenging to move from Wenger's general approach to more concrete practices that help teachers develop effective learning relationships. Wenger sees effective learning relationships as a social or organizational phenomenon of belonging, and he presents personal motivation as a process of identification with valued practices of a learning community. He argues that students are not motivated to learn per se but are motivated to belong to a specific enterprise of a community of practice. Students are not as driven to learn as they are driven to belong to a worthy project. As a result of relational and practical concerns, students enter effective learning relationships. They learn to do something with others.

Wenger's framework is further explicated by the role of dialogue in learning and relating. The root of the term *dialogue* is related to a dialectical opposition of perspectives in search of *truth*. Unlike discussions that are generally a linear process of building ideas upon ideas, dialogue suggests an exchange or transaction of differing ideas. Hans-Georg Gadamer's (1989) concept of dialogue actualizes Wenger's communities of practice and provides a teaching method for engaging students and transforming their ideas and thinking. Gadamer sees learning as interpersonal and intrapersonal competence that emerges between persons in dialogue. To Gadamer, learning happens in a process of conversing with other people about a subject matter or task at hand. Like Wenger, Gadamer's approach does not primarily focus on the individual acquisition of information but on learners engaging with other people's concepts, testing one's concepts against those of others, and recognizing productive from nonproductive prejudices and opinions.

Gadamer's concept of dialogue becomes the foundation of a community of practice. Dialogue is a method whereby students participate in a conversation that moves between the individual and the community. Each person in the dialogue brings a perspective to the community. Gadamer describes the process as a "circle of understanding" that moves back and forth from the group to the student and back again. One example of the circular movement is the process of reading. When a student reads a sentence (the part) of a book (the whole), what has already been learned puts the sentence into a new perspective. Likewise, when the student develops a new understanding of the sentence, the whole context or understanding of the book is enhanced. The same thing happens in a dialogue with other people. There is a circular interaction that is holistic, not linear. Learning is not a movement from point to point but a circular dynamic between the parts and the whole, or between the individual and the community.

On the other hand, Gadamer's notion of dialogue is not a vicious circle that moves thinking in circles but one that advances thought. The circle of understanding is a hermeneutic circle that is different in that it is constantly augmented by a dialectical practice of exchanging logical arguments. Hermeneutic understanding progresses by a cross-examination of claims that draw out contradictions and inconsistencies. The ultimate task of the circle of understanding is the testing of ideas to arrive at a practical understanding. Gadamer recognizes that learners get stuck in a vicious circle only if they are entrenched in their own opinions and do not try to understand. Learning always begins with students projecting unexamined biases or prejudices. There is no other starting point. *Prejudices* are not always false judgments and can have a positive value. But they always require testing in dialogue. In dialogue, learners become aware of their own biases and then a subject matter can be addressed in all of its complexity.

In dialogue, students learn to be open to the perspectives of other people. When they practice openness, they consider meanings contrary to their present beliefs. They share their prejudices, compare them to another person's vantage point, and consider new understandings. They maintain their present perspective, or "horizon of experience," only if the other person's ideas do not stand up to facts or logic.

Gadamer's concept of dialogue is attuned to the complexities of Wenger's communities of practice and effective learning relationships. He recognizes that learning and relationships are enhanced when there is a sharing of prejudices within a community of people committed to a common endeavor. When prejudices and ideas are clarified by members of a community, individuals get the opportunity to learn who they are and who they may want to be. In this way, students in a classroom community can critically construct meaning and form identities. They learn the complexities of authentic learning and the role of vantage points. Consequently, they are in better position to decide what they believe, what kind of people they will become, and what collective endeavors are of value to them.

Fusion of Horizons

Wenger's ideas of doing things together, entering communities of practice, and collectively creating meaning are further reflected in Gadamer's idea of a *fusion of horizons*. To Gadamer, when learning happens and present horizons of experience are moved to new understandings by an encounter in dialogue, both horizons are combined into something new of living value—a transformation. Like Wenger, Gadamer sees education as not primarily techniques that deliver curriculum and transmit knowledge, but as relationships that reconstruct meaning and identities together. For example, an openly gay student in one of my classes was very willing to share who he was and his experiences with the attitudes and feelings of others. The subject matter of the class was teaching, communication, and diversity, so it was relevant for him to enter into dialogue about the subject with classmates. It was not an easy conversation for everyone. One student would not even look him in the eyes. But the majority of students in class were motivated not simply to learn teaching techniques but to become teachers in diverse situations. The tone of the conversation was authentic interest in understanding. They all knew that one day they would have to deal with diverse students in their classes.

They had sense of a common endeavor and community that clarified the need for openness, dialogue, and understanding. Ultimately, they learned about another person, about themselves, and about communication in challenging situations.

Effective learning relationships are not simply about interactions where one person's intention, including a teacher's, directs the conversation. They are not focused on the vantage point of any one person. There is a fusion of horizons. In the process, teachers and students become caught up in something larger than their individual intentions. The dialogical structure of effective learning relationships replaces any absolute distinction between teacher and student. It places the focus on the subject between those in dialogue. Learning is neither completely teacher- nor student-centered but becomes a structural unity. Learning is a relational process that emerges between individuals.

Effective learning relationships lead to a fusion of horizons or *transformation* between people. If a teacher and student are open, they are willing not only to share information but to develop identities together. Openness permits them to take in the claims of the other person, to bounce one's prejudices against the other, and to come to a new understanding of the subject matter. Learning becomes a mediation of horizons—teacher and student alike. There is a shared blending of understanding and a transformation of the initial positions of each person. In fact, a new understanding is produced where no one person can take full credit. Effective learning relationships add something of value to each person's horizon. Authentic dialogue between people helps to create communication, relationship, and understanding.

Figure 5.1 illustrates how communication and learning are communal—a bringing together of horizons. Personal views are informed by critical dialogue, merge with another's view, and produce new horizons of meaning. The old horizons of each person combine into a new understanding, or fusion of horizons. A fusion of horizons is fundamental to doing things together and a useful image for what happens in teaching and learning. When teachers and students interact, all horizons change. Communication produces a fusion that transforms people and creates community. Horizons of experience, sharing of prejudices, and dialogue all contribute to a fusion of horizons—the basis of communities of practice and effective learning relationships.

Of course, students do not simply drop old horizons and enter into new understandings, relationships, and community. They need help from a teacher to open up new horizons and to "try on" new behaviors. Consequently, it is important for teachers to remember that students always have their own horizons. It's part of identity development. Teaching involves both content and peoplemaking. Teachers structure learning and community in order to help students share assumptions and prejudices appropriately. By doing this, teachers encourage student transfor-

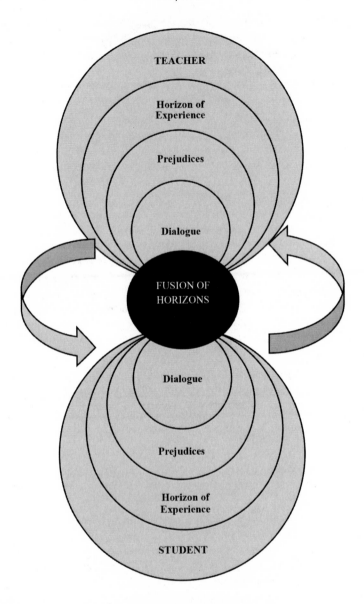

Figure 5.1.   Fusion of Horizons and Teacher Communication.

mations. Effective learning relationships are fundamental to this transformation.

CHALLENGES TO EFFECTIVE LEARNING RELATIONSHIPS

As Wenger observes, common interest in a valued enterprise provides the basis for effective learning relationships. Gadamer adds that dialogue and fusions of horizons help build effective learning relationships with people who think quite differently. On the other hand, it is only natural that challenges and conflicts arise when teachers attempt to develop effective learning relationships with students, parents, and colleagues. One possible challenge is the diversity of culture, ethnic backgrounds, and race in contemporary schools. Years ago, white, Anglo-Saxon, Protestant males dominated positions of authority in most public high schools, and white, Anglo-Saxon, Protestant females dominated teaching positions in most elementary schools. Today there is more diversity at all levels. High schools hire more women, and there are more male teachers at the elementary level. In addition, schools employ a higher percentage of ethnic and racial minorities.

In today's schools, teachers face the challenge of promoting effective learning relationships in a very diverse environment. If a teacher maintains a detached attitude toward diversity, he or she risks not being able to establish the authentic social interaction, dialogue, and identity construction necessary for effective learning relationships. Differences are a rich resource for true dialogue, and effective learning relationships depend on the exchanges of those differences. People with different backgrounds, skills, attitudes, and experiences bring fresh ideas and perceptions. Differences are harnessed to make dialogue relevant, and they draw upon the widest possible range of views.

Teachers who are willing to face the diversity challenge take advantage of the major attitude change that has taken place in our country. For many years, Americans saw diversity as a "melting pot" and promoted a single language, culture, and a common tradition. Today, they see diversity as a "salad bowl" where a nation is created out of different cultures, traditions, and lifestyles—all united by common beliefs like freedom and democracy. Within the "salad bowl" view, teachers can look beyond outward appearances and accept cultural, ethnic, or racial differences. They can see all students as unique, thinking, and feeling individuals.

Confronting diversity challenges to effective learning relationships gives teachers the opportunity to recognize their own horizons and prejudices as well. Hidden prejudices can control a teacher's attitudes and behaviors. Because of status and power in the classroom, teachers can believe that they are free of prejudices and not see the need for dialogue with students. They miss significant learning opportunities. Taking advantage of these opportunities does not always make it easy to communicate with students. Authentic dialogue exposes prejudices of which teachers may not be aware. When teachers are open and willing to risk dialogue, they invest in effective learning relationships.

A second possible challenge to building effective learning relationships is sexism. Like other professions, teaching involves communication with sexual undertones. Sexual references are not necessarily problematic and may have little influence on teacher communication one way or the other. But that's not always the case. Sometimes sexual language undermines relationships and positive attitudes. It doesn't take long for awkward relationships to develop, and effective learning relationships with colleagues begin to suffer.

Before sexual language undermines communication and relationships in a school, warning signs are usually present. For example, one warning sign is when an administrator dates a teacher in his or her own school. There is immediate suspicion of favoritism. It is likewise when two teachers date and do not keep their private and public worlds separate, or when teachers are apparently in an intimate relationship outside of their marriages.

One form of sexism, sexual harassment, involves behavior of a sexual nature that causes school employees to feel uncomfortable and has a negative impact on professional relationships. Sexual harassment is intentional and comes in three main forms:

- Verbal and/or oral communication—Telling risqué jokes in the lunchroom, commenting on another teacher's anatomy, pursuing an unreciprocated relationship, or asking for sexual favors.
- Visual communication—Wearing clothing that does not fit the standards of the school, staring at someone's anatomy, or flirting nonverbally.
- Physical communication—Touching, standing too close, giving a too-lengthy handshake, or initiating excessive hugging.

Sexual harassment violates the law, inhibits teacher performance, and undermines any potential for effective learning relationships. The problem needs to move to a formal arena. If a teacher believes he or she is being sexually harassed, a complaint can be made to the principal or human resources officer with the specific times of the harassment documented. If the source of the harassment happens to be someone with authority over the victim, a union representative might need to be contacted.

Sexism also influences the ability to create effective learning relationships in the classroom through *gender bias*—sexism through curriculum, educational materials, and classroom interaction. The American association of University Women (1992) and Christina Sommers (2002) argue that bias affects both boys and girls in the classroom. For example, female students often receive less attention, encouragement, and serious regard than their male counterparts. Male students, on the other hand, continue to experience lower grades, more suspensions, and labeling as learning disabled or emotionally disturbed.

A major issue around gender bias in the classroom is classroom interaction. Studies show that male and female students experience classroom interaction differently. Lea Stewart and colleagues (2003) observe that male students who are straightforward and unreserved get more teacher attention, praise, academic help, and acceptance of ideas and opinions during classroom discussions. Under such bias, students cannot learn objectively about a subject matter, about themselves, and about relating to people of other genders. Learning is enabled through objective and equitable interaction. Equal opportunity is a fundamental part of effective learning relationships.

A third possible challenge to building effective learning relationships is *ageism*. Ageism involves stereotyping and discriminating against individuals or groups on the basis of age. It can be informal or systematic, involving prejudicial attitudes, discriminatory practices, and institutional policies that perpetuate stereotypes about age.

Ageism is also used to describe discrimination against younger teachers, including ignoring their ideas because of their age and lack of experience. For example, new teachers are often faced with the challenge of ageism in most schools. Although teachers in their late twenties and early thirties consider youth as an advantage for relating to students, many school cultures expect beginning teachers to "pay their dues" before their talents and skills are recognized. Consequently, young teachers feel a generation gap. They want to be taken seriously and to feel part of the school, but ageism is a problem for them when trying to develop effective learning relationships with more seasoned teachers.

Beginning teachers can act in response to ageism. They can show that they can accept and handle responsibility. They can do research and make informed decisions that enhance personal credibility. They can intentionally build effective learning relationships with older teachers. Most experienced teachers will not resist a beginning teacher's efforts if approached in the right way. They are often willing to help.

There are also advantages for experienced teachers to building effective learning relationships with younger colleagues. All teachers like to receive recognition. Veteran teachers are the same. They want to feel important as professionals and people. They want to feel appreciated and to receive credit when due. In addition, many seasoned teachers want to keep a contemporary image and be relevant. Any action by a new teacher that helps an older teacher to feel "in touch" is helpful. In return, a new teacher learns a lot. Beginning teachers benefit from any effort to keep communication lines with experienced teachers open and to get advice about teaching-related issues.

Seasoned teachers benefit from relationships with new teachers by being exposed to fresh ideas and contagious energy. Consequently, experienced teachers can take steps to develop effective learning relationships as well. Three actions appreciated by new teachers are:

- Showing patience with beginning teachers' adjustment,
- Sharing experiences helpful to new teachers, and
- Providing encouragement for young teachers to communicate.

CONCLUSION

Effective learning relationships enhance a teacher's ability to help students learn about a subject matter, about themselves, and about relating to others. Relational teacher communication promotes a sense of community, participation, belonging, and dialogue, fundamental ingredients for effective learning relationships. Through effective learning relationships, students become part of a community of practice and valued educational endeavors.

SIX

Communicating with Parents

> Effective communication is essential for building school-family partnerships. It constitutes the foundation for all other forms of family involvement in education. — *American Federation of Teachers*

This chapter discusses communication between a teacher and parents. It shows how communication with parents includes both command and relational skills and builds effective learning relationships. Although it recognizes that current parent-teacher relationships are strong (NEA, 2012), it also shows how many of the frustrations that teachers experience with parents result from focusing on command communication and not on effective learning relationships. Effective communication with parents requires a sense of community, peoplemaking, and dialogue, including a circle of understanding and a fusion of horizons. The chapter presents a range of communication guidelines and methods for teachers to build effective learning relationships with parents, including communication through technology.

Cultivating a community of practice with parents is vital to productive teacher–parent relationships. Research shows that most parents appreciate effective communication with teachers, especially messages that contain constructive suggestions for student improvement and academic success. Unfortunately, as Sara Lawrence-Lightfoot (2004) recognizes, many teachers are not trained to communicate effectively with parents and build partnerships. Effective teacher training requires the development of relational communication skills. This chapter presents a range of teacher communication strategies and skills that encourage a sense of community, dialogue, and partnership with parents.

FUNCTIONS OF TEACHER–PARENT COMMUNICATION

Effective teacher–parent communication functions in a couple ways. Charles Conrad's (2012) two functions of command and relational communication are especially relevant to teacher–parent interaction. Command communication occurs when teachers inform parents about events, activities, or student progress through a variety of means such as email, newsletters, report cards, and websites. On the other hand, relational communication is about the quality of communication between the teacher and parents. Dialogue needs to be encouraged during phone calls, home visits, teacher–parent conferences, open houses, and other school-based community events. Teachers can actively incorporate both command and relational communication to maximize sharing information and understanding with parents.

Command Function of Teacher–Parent Communication

Teachers communicate at the command level when they send messages to parents in clearly prescribed ways. Written communication is probably the most efficient and effective way teachers provide clear information to parents. Written messages address any and all parents. They make information official and are written in a formal capacity. A written command is a relatively permanent injunction and addresses issues and problems that are important and recurring.

Written messages emphasize teacher clarity. A teacher sends information to parents clearly and concisely. Messages require careful consideration regarding format and content. A teacher intends for parents to easily read and understand the information. Examples of written command communication include newsletters and brochures that share information with parents. Clarity is enhanced by using everyday language, avoiding educational jargon, and increasing readability. Clarity is also increased through proper grammar, spell-check, and proofreading the information.

Oral instructions are examples of command communication given in face-to-face encounters with parents. Oral messages are more situational and flexible and are transient rather than permanent. They are linked to specific student problems that are relatively new, rare, or unprecedented. In the case of oral instructions, a teacher decides it is more important to deliver the instructions in a face-to-face meeting with parents rather than through a written exchange. For example, a student may be having difficulty with a specific assignment and it is problematic to give clear, concise written instructions to parents about how to help the student. The teacher wants the opportunity to respond immediately to parents' questions.

Relational Function of Teacher–Parent Communication

The dynamics of teacher–parent interaction often make teacher communication considerably more challenging than simply dealing with official, one-way commands. Teacher–parent communication is not always rational. It is made up of living, thinking, and emotional human beings — actors who constantly make choices and are not inanimate objects. Effective teacher–parent communication is not solely command-oriented; it is also an important medium for relational communication. In the relational realm, horizons and emotions, not tasks or logical sequences, are the significant factors within which teachers communicate. Instead of depending solely on clarity and precision, teacher–parent communication requires working with uncertainty and interpretations. If teachers adjust to this less rational process, communication can be more effective with parents and give structure to confusing information.

Relational communication is the basis of effective learning relationships and enables the development of communities of practice, dialogue and fusions of horizons. It encourages mutuality of concern and appreciation of contrasting perspectives and requires interpersonal skills. It needs a quality of communication with parents that can be present in a variety of situations, including on the phone or in face-to-face teacher–parent conferences. All communication situations with parents are possible arenas for interpersonal interaction. Using interpersonal communication is a choice that teachers can make in all kinds of situations.

Three questions help teachers to make the decision to be more or less interpersonal with parents: (1) Does it help communication to focus on what makes a parent feel unique? (2) Does it help communication to respect a parent's ability to think and make choices? (3) Does it help communication to pay attention to a parent's feelings?

Parents are unique.

Parents are never interchangeable. They have unique past experiences with school, some positive and some negative. They may or may not bring a "chip on their shoulder" regarding school. They are in different kinds of relationships — married, traditional, same-sex, divorced, single. They have a variety of personal interests. They hold a diversity of religious, spiritual, and philosophical beliefs. They show different personality traits and physical characteristics. Finally, they have a variety of natural talents, some very helpful when thye volunteer in the classroom.

Parents judge school situations and their child's performance according to their own horizons of experience — past school experiences, culture, faith, and values — all of which help formulate current beliefs about teachers and school in general. The meanings that parents give to school are based on their core beliefs and prejudices.

Parents think and make choices.

Many parents encourage their children to ask questions, and they are not afraid to acknowledge that they do not have all the answers. They welcome the opportunity for their children to explore various answers. Consequently, it is crucial for a teacher to understand how parents think and the way they analyze problems and discover solutions. If parents are open to collaborative problem-solving, a teacher can encourage a partnership where parents contribute responses to issues, solutions to problems, and useful questions, comments, and answers. Encouragement is important. When teachers encourage parents to participate, they help to develop a more collaborative relationship about solving problems. One way to encourage parents is by asking them to share a response in more detail or to "say more." This invites parents to collaborate more fully in educational decisions and possible solutions.

Parents have feelings.

Discussing a child's school performance often stirs up strong parental feelings. It is common for parents to feel that they are not doing everything they could or that they are not "good" parents. They worry that others are better at parenting than they are. Teachers must deal with the strong feelings of parents. Teacher responses carry great weight. A miscalculated response can backfire, fan the flames of a parent's feelings, and make it harder to build relational communication.

When teachers face a challenging encounter with parental feelings, they can get things back on track and provide the best guidance for a student. First, teachers can assess their own feelings. If teachers are not aware of their own feelings, hidden emotions can interfere with building a strong and positive relationship with parents. Second, teachers should look at interactions from parents' point of view. Increasing empathy can lead to a more collaborative approach. If parents feel incompetent and embarrassed, a teacher can reframe the issue in order to help parents feel better and understand the complexity of the issue.

Teacher–parent partnerships help to develop solution-based plans when teachers and parents collaborate rather than compete. Teachers invite parental perspectives to clarify feelings and beliefs about an issue. Teachers ask questions to learn and to not pass judgment. They encourage parental ideas and discover where the teacher and parents agree and how the teacher and parents can work together.

Jesus Acosta and colleagues (2015) offer teachers a framework for developing solution-based methods for working with parents. They call it L.E.A.P. First, teachers listen to parents actively. As described in chapter 1, active *listening* involves paraphrasing and perception-checking. Second, teachers *empathize* with the feelings of parents. This consists of teachers acknowledging a parent's feelings and verifying those feelings with statements such as, "I can see you are very upset." Third, teachers *ask* questions to understand a parent's perspective. Authentic questions do not reflect a teacher's agenda but search for a parent's ideas and emotions. Fourth, teachers *problem-solve* by evaluating a current problem and determining a practical plan for solving the problem. The L.E.A.P. mindset requires teacher openness to parents' ideas, to cooperating with parents, and to coming up with a practical plan.

Like everyone, parents do not appreciate a cold, professional approach from people they work with. Teachers who focus on a personal touch and interpersonal communication can enhance relationships with parents. Whenever teachers communicate with parents, they have the opportunity to fuse horizons. They have a peoplemaking opportunity and can help parents reach new understandings. Teacher communication plays a profound role in helping parents become better educators. Teachers benefit from the experience and wisdom of transformed parents.

Communicating through Technology

Relational communication between teachers and parents is challenging. Both teachers and parents are busy, and it is hard to make human connections. Integrating technology into the process can help teachers to communicate relationally with parents and create a community of practice. It can enhance relational communication and encourage dialogue between teachers and parents. It can help overcome the challenges of schedules, time, and distance.

Susan Ramasubbu (2015) suggests a series of questions to help teachers decide whether technology is appropriate for parent communication and, if so, which type of technology should be used. Selection is based on responses to the following questions:

- What is the nature of the message to be communicated? Is it private? Or is it intended for a parent community?
- What technology is available to both teacher and parent? Is there a digital divide? Many families living in poverty do not have access to the Internet.
- What are the levels of skills and willingness for both teachers and parents to use technology? Some teachers only have access to email and are not comfortable communicating on social networks such as Facebook.
- Will the technology complement or complicate communication? As chapter 12 will point out, communicating online can be interpersonal. But sometimes a situation requires face-to-face interaction. A problem may be sensitive, and any give-and-take between teacher and parent is going to involve pauses and a search for words.

Once a teacher decides to use technology to communicate with parents, there are a number of options.

Cell phones

Cell phone calls to parents can be convenient, proactive, and have more interpersonal impact than a written message. When a student's performance makes an unusual slip, a phone call can give parents the chance to acclimate themselves to what they will be discussing in more detail later. It also gives teachers the chance to give parents immediate suggestions about how they can help improve a child's performance and even "nip the issue in the bud."

Email

Teachers can use email to send letters, notes, files, data, or reports all using the same techniques. Once a teacher learns how to use email, everything can be sent the same way. Teachers don't have to worry about interrupting a parent through email. Parents can deal with email messages at a convenient time. They don't have to stop what they are doing when email arrives. Teachers can also send email at a convenient time for themsleves. It doesn't have to be written or sent at a time when a teacher knows the parent will be available. This is asynchronous communication. Parents can become virtually engaged in an ongoing conversation about their child's performance and behavior in class.

Web Pages

Web pages are probably the best technology for creating an electronic community of practice for parents. Teachers provide information and updates on class activities on a regular basis. Progress reports and grades are disseminated. Students can participate by taking responsibility for particular sections of the Web page and displaying their work. Parents can check the site each day and participate in online conversations with a teacher and other parents. Web pages invite participation and a sense of belonging to a community. Effective learning relationships are reflected in technological communities of practice. Parents experience a sense of belonging to a "commonwealth" through engagement and connection with other parents.

Video Technology

Videos can make parents feel more included in their child's education. Teachers can create short videos posted on a Web page that welcome parents to school and invite their involvement. A teacher gives a short introduction to the goals of the class or a tour of the school. Videos can be tailored to particular assignments or projects. They can show parents how to facilitate a science project. A teacher can use video to illustrate how to do complicated math problems.

Social Networking Tools

Social networking sites and apps like Facebook, Snapchat, Instagram, Edmodo, YouTube, and Vine can be dicey. School districts often restrict teacher involvement with such tools, and there have been plenty of examples of teachers sharing inappropriate information online. Teachers are discouraged from "friending" students on Facebook and are held to a higher standard than people in many other professions. This is for good reason. Being friends with a student often leads to a breakdown of the teacher–student relationship. Students who use a teacher's first name may misinterpret it as being that teacher's friend.

But online tools have a place in parent communication. For example, a Facebook page can be used for keeping parents up on student progress and activities. It keeps alive a sense of collaboration in a community of practice. Facebook has created a special feature called "groups for schools." Teachers share files, create events, and help parents stay current about what's happening in class. Parents are part of a group using a helpful place for them to find out about school events and homework assignments. YouTube is also a great social media platform for education. Many teachers use the site for showing videos at home to students with their parents.

Technology allows teacher–parent communication to not be limited by time or space. And it can be practical, positive, and interpersonal. Technological tools can be efficient means to enhance teacher–parent communication and allow teachers, parents, and students to stay connected and informed in a community of practice.

PARENTS AND EFFECTIVE LEARNING RELATIONSHIPS

Elena Aguilar (2015) understands that teachers need to appreciate the elements and characteristics of effective parent communication and know how to encourage it. They need to understand the means for improving parent communication skills. This next section provides specific ways for creating effective learning relationships with parents.

Many schools set clear goals for increasing family engagement and reaching parents. More than information about the school or classroom, the goals are intended to increase parents' participation and sense of belonging. They encourage parents to engage information and share in doing things with others. Teachers are also in the business of peoplemaking with parents in order to create coeducators. To do this, teachers need to increase parental participation in the valued enterprise of educating their children. Parental interaction and a sense of belonging are central.

Teachers who want a plan for improving teacher–parent communication and for developing effective learning relationships with parents should heed the following suggestions.

Develop Goals

The basic strategy for developing effective teacher–parent communication is having clear communication goals. Teachers should not communicate with parents simply because they think they should. Teacher–parent communication should be tied to a teacher's goals in the classroom. Does the teacher want students to have better attendance? Does a teacher want more parent volunteers to cover increasing responsibilities around standardized testing? How will communication help satisfy specific goals? Will communication with parents help create a community of practice and encourage productive teacher–parent–student relationships? Will goals include a log and documentation of communication interactions with parents?

Know Your Students

Before teachers communicate with parents about students' needs, they must know about students' interests, learning profiles, and readiness to learn. There are many tools to help teachers learn about the individuals in their classrooms. Teachers can learn student names and ask questions about students. What kinds of things and activities do they enjoy? Who are the special people in their lives? Who are the members of their family? What do they think is their best characteristic? What do they need to succeed in school? What are some obstacles to school success? Teachers can learn student likes and dislikes and how to keep them engaged in learning. Teachers can learn to tell when a student is upset and how to help. They can learn how to see when a student is struggling or when someone is being bullied.

Parents are the greatest resource about their child. Teachers can openly solicit suggestions about how to better serve their child. Teachers can offer ideas and activities that parents can do at home to enhance the learning process.

Build Community

Teachers should invite communication with parents early. Susan Graham-Clay (2015) sees strong communication as fundamental to building a sense of community between school and home. By using technology mentioned above—email, Web pages, phone calls, newsletters, notes to home—teachers encourage parental communication and participation. They make it clear that they value parents' questions, want to create a positive atmosphere, and wish parents to participate. It is very useful for teachers to find out about the knowledge and skills of parents. With this information, teachers can connect parental involvement with curriculum and content. Teachers can also encourage parents to share their cultural traditions. This invites diverse participation and a sense of belonging. In addition, teachers should greet parents with a smile when they come to class and be clear about what parent volunteers will be doing in class. Knowing what is expected increases a parent's sense of purpose.

Teachers can invite parents to participate in making decisions about the classroom. They can give parents information to help them form opinions about the workings of the class. Afterwards, teachers listen to the parents' conclusions and thank them. Parents get recognition for how they are helping in class and how important it is to students. A community of practice is strengthened when teachers and parents share information and decisions.

Conduct Positive Conferences

The most critical incident in teacher–parent communication is the parent–teacher conference. It is also the most significant interpersonal communication event and deserves special attention. The goal of the conference is two-fold: (1) to discuss and respond to a student's progress and (2) to develop an effective learning relationship with the parent. To understand a student's performance, a teacher needs to know about a child's home life. For example, would it be more productive for divorced parents to have separate conferences?

The teacher should pay attention to the physical structure of the conference. Proxemics, or spatial relations, are particularly important. To set a more interpersonal tone, distance between parent and teacher should be "personal," eighteen inches to four feet. Another issue regards open versus closed seating design. Physical barriers like desks or chairs between parent and teacher tend to be more impersonal. Parents feel more welcome and comfortable in conferences with open design. They view teachers as more immediate, friendly, and helpful.

When discussing student progress with parents, teachers should begin with positive comments about the student. This sets a productive tone. Even student oppositional behavior can be put into a positive framework by sharing with a parent that the behavior indicates a sense of independence. At any rate, initial positive comments put parents into a receptive attitude about areas where the student needs to improve.

When the conference about student performance turns to questions of improvement, teacher-initiated dialogue helps maintain an effective learning relationship. A solution-based approach finds specific things that will improve student performance and invites parent participation. Of course, teachers can have responses, rather than answers, prepared for this part of the interaction. Authentic dialogue between parent and teacher can lead to shared responses and a fusion of horizons. Before teachers offer responses, though, they should encourage parents to express their ideas about what actions they think will improve the student's progress. Teachers listen, paraphrase, and check perceptions in order to understand the parents' perspective. If there is a lull in the conversation, teachers can then offer responses for consideration. If parents respond positively, the ideas can be pursued.

Ultimately, the goal is to generate a plan for improvement that contains ideas that spring from the interaction between parents and teacher. The plan and ideas then reflect an effective learning relationship between teachers and parents.

CONCLUSION

Today's teachers should be skilled in the art of teaching and in the art of communicating with parents. Effective teacher–parent communication is essential to parental involvement and student success. This chapter described a number of communication opportunities and strategies that help parents become informed participants in their child's education. They all include the human touch. Teacher–parent communication should reflect a thoughtful, planned, and humane approach for teachers to promote parental collaboration and to support student learning.

SEVEN

Communicating with a Principal

> Relationships among teachers and principals, in particular, are being
> held out as important indicators of a school's or district's readiness for
> reform and ability to sustain it. —*Cori Brewster and Jennifer Railsback,*
> *Northwest Regional Educational Laboratory*

This chapter discusses communication between teachers and principals.
Like communication with parents, effective teacher communication with
principals involves building effective learning relationships. And like
with parents, strong communication with principals requires building a
community of practice, a sense of partnership, and a fusion of horizons.
The chapter outlines the communication styles of principals and the relationship between those styles and teacher responses. It describes some
qualities and skills of today's principals, and it presents teachers with a
range of communication guidelines to help build effective learning relationships with principals.

Developing communities of practice is an important part of effective
learning relationships with principals. They are also an important part of
school reform. Cori Brewster and Jennifer Railsback (2003) show that
schools with little or no sense of community (trust) have little or no
chance of improving school, teacher, and student practice. There is also a
connection between the level of community in a school and student learning. In this context, Mary Alice Anderson (2002) sees the most important
relationship teachers must deal with is the one between them and their
principal. This single relationship contributes to either building community and speeding up school improvement or slowing both down. It
makes teaching either a joy or a drag. It prepares teachers for new tasks
associated with school reform, or it leads to teacher frustrations. There is
no way to avoid the fact that teachers must cope with their principals.

WHO IS TODAY'S PRINCIPAL?

It is impossible to describe the kind of principal teachers will have in any particular school. The hope is that he or she has teaching experience and uses that experience in administrative responsibilities. Daniel Smith (2013) recognizes that principals vary in the kinds and levels of training that help them be good principals. A principal may be easy to get along with or difficult. He or she may be sensitive or insensitive to teacher needs. A principal may be feeling his or her way along and making mistakes, or a principal may be highly experienced.

Principals cannot be clearly classified into different groups. Each principal has a unique personality. Each has a unique style. The qualities and skills of principals have changed over the past few years, but three things are certain about today's principal: (1) principals have an obligation to know, walk, and talk effective teaching; (2) principals need to play a key role in the planning, implementation, and evaluation of professional teaching; and (3) principals require effective communication skills.

A principal serves a number of important communication roles. First, a principal is a *teacher*. The way a principal communicates, or teaches, has a great influence on teacher attitude toward responsibilities and the school. Teachers can learn from a principal's reservoir of knowledge, skills, and techniques. Teachers are most fortunate if a principal is a good communicator. Second, a principal is a *mentor*. A principal's job is to see that teachers perform to their potential, and they help teachers develop skills and correct teaching behaviors. If a principal is too detached, it can hinder the mentoring process. Teachers are better off with concerned principals. With a concerned principal who takes the time to train, teachers can improve. A principal needs to communicate effectively about improving teaching performance and have heart-to-heart talks with teachers.

Finally, a principal is a *leader*. Principals must provide a productive style, set a positive communication climate for a school, and motivate teachers. Kurt Lewin and colleagues (1939) conducted leadership decision experiments in 1939 and identified three different styles of leadership particularly useful as the bases of communication climates. Teachers need to have a sense of the principal's style and the particular communication climate it creates. It is beneficial for teachers to "fit" into a communication climate. The following descriptions of the various kinds of leadership styles and communication climates give teachers an indication of the adjustments needed to work with a principal and fit within a school organization.

The Structured or Autocratic Principal

When comfortable in a structured or autocratic communication climate, principals tend to make decisions without consulting teachers. They operate a tight school by keeping a close eye on things. They expect teachers to be on time, orderly, and highly efficient. They are informal only when the occasion calls for it but otherwise stick strictly to business.

Principals who show an autocratic style often appear cold, distant, and unfeeling. They may also seem unreachable. As a result, new teachers may be reluctant to approach this type of principal. Although principals who establish this kind of climate appear indifferent and unapproachable, the opposite can be true. They may be more interested and willing to help than new teachers suspect.

In fact, sometimes an autocratic style and climate are necessary. Principals in decision-making positions may not have the opportunity to be open to change and teacher input. Some jobs and responsibilities require very strict safety standards or efficiency. For example, principals need to adhere to the requirements of state standardized testing. School boards may need to focus primarily on high-stakes test scores and require structured principals who can "right the ship." Responsibilities of this nature, where certain standards must be met, call for a structured climate.

The Permissive, or Laissez-Faire, Principal

The direct opposite of the structured principal is the permissive, or laissez-faire, principal. This style minimizes a principal's involvement in decision-making and encourages teachers to make the decisions. Of course, principals vary on the level of permissiveness. Technically, laissez-faire leadership involves an absence of leadership styles, but it can be anywhere on a continuum between no leadership (laissez-faire) and minimal leadership (permissive).

The laissez-faire style can be problematic, especially for inexperienced teachers. A new teacher may not get valuable guidance from a principal. The teacher may find it difficult to develop self-direction about issues of discipline, organization, and teaching methods. If things are too easygoing, a new teacher may become too informal with students and too centered on student "friendships" than on professional responsibilities. This can lead to tensions and ultimately parental dissatisfaction. Laissez-faire climates can damage a new teacher's chances of success if he or she raises too many concerns. Sometimes a more structured climate offers beginning teachers clearer boundaries for professional development and forces them to live closer to their teaching potential.

On the other hand, a permissive climate works if teachers are capable and motivated to make their own decisions. A permissive style requires highly trained and reliable teachers who principals trust to make appropriate decisions. The roles of teachers in laissez-faire environments can involve self-monitoring, problem-solving, and developing successful learning outcomes. Permissive principals are most successful with highly self-directed teachers.

The Democratic, or Facilitative, Principal

A democratic style is where principals involve teachers and parents in shared decision-making. The decision-making process may vary from principals having the final say to principals building consensus. Democratic principals try to motivate teachers to want to do what is best. They become one of the group and encourage teachers to have a say about the operation of the school. Democratic principals strive to move away from an authoritarian style to a more relational enterprise. As this book has discussed, productivity and positive relationships are closely linked in school organizations. If principals treat teachers with dignity and move the communication to a more collegial atmosphere, they help teachers to reach performance goals rather than force them to do so.

A democratic or facilitative style encourages participation and a sense of belonging. It promotes teachers to achieve better outcomes if they participate in setting goals and directing efforts. The style assumes that under the proper communication climate, teachers motivate themselves. Like communities of practice, everyone is involved by working from inside the group rather than from outside. A principal is a leader and member of the group at the same time. Consequently, a team feeling and sense of belonging are created. Most teachers experience greater personal satisfaction and better performance when principals create and maintain a democratic teaching environment.

An example of democratic leadership in school is *site-based management*. Site-based management (1994) is a way of reforming school leadership so that teachers and parents have more management responsibility. While it shifts decision-making from the central authority of a school board or superintendent to the local school's staff and parents, it also shifts decision-making from the principal to teachers and parents. Site-based management recognizes that student learning is improved when decisions are moved closer to home and classrooms. Decisions involve groups, stakeholders, and parents. Ideally, the principal in site-based management becomes a sort of executive director who provides information and advice to the site council.

Depending on the levels of principal, teacher, and parent involvement, the site council can be a meaningful or menial experience. Site-based management challenges principals to accept and achieve democratic leadership and communication. It is the most difficult communication climate to maintain. It requires principals with skill, sensitivity, and humility. It is also difficult to find a large number of principals with this communication and organizational ability.

Not all teachers and parents respond positively to a democratic climate, though. There are teachers who wish principals would "tighten things up around here." They don't enjoy working for a principal who doesn't set things down clearly and specifically from the beginning. It is also a question of accountability. Some teachers and parents want the principal to be clearly accountable, not one council member among many who shares accountability.

Teachers and parents may also want principals to create and maintain a discipline line. Like in a classroom, this is an imaginary point beyond which teachers should not pass without the threat of disapproval or disciplinary action. It helps principals keep consistent discipline in line. Keeping an orderly but comfortable environment is a tightrope many democratic principals walk each day on the job.

The Transformational Principal

There is a fourth style that needs to be added to Lewin's perspective. John Hoyle (2012) argues that *transformational* leaders create a communication climate where every person is empowered to become a better person who fulfills his or her highest professional and personal needs. Transformational principals see themselves as serving others and guiding teachers, parents, and students to top performance. They see a cause beyond themselves, and they promote inclusiveness for people of different cultures, ethnic backgrounds, race, gender, and ages. They do this by encouraging dialogue and being open to a fusion of horizons.

Like Hans-Georg Gadamer's perspective, Heather Price's (2012) transformational principals see learning as emerging between people. For them, dialogue is a communication method for gaining understanding and for peoplemaking. There is an interrelation between dialogue and identity. Teachers, parents, and students are transformed through dialogue. Reflecting Gadamer's fusion of horizons, transformational principals encourage people to move to new horizons of understanding by encounters in dialogue. Through dialogue and a fusion of horizons, a community of practice emerges. A sense of common endeavor is created, and teachers learn about community, about themselves, and about how to communicate across differences. Besides being a useful metaphor for the learning process, dialogue is a metaphor for transformational communication.

WHAT CAN TEACHERS DO?

Every principal contributes to a communication climate. Some principals come up with a workable blend of structured and democratic styles. Others come up with a blend of democratic and permissive styles. Some are transformational. Whether teachers like a principal's style is not the issue. Teachers must learn to fit within the communication climate the principal helps to create. A teacher should not be too quick to judge. What appears to be a difficult communication climate at the beginning might turn out to be a comfortable and beneficial one later. Whatever the style of the principal, a teacher's responsibility is to build the best possible effective learning relationship with the principal. J.A. Peoples (1964) long established that teacher communication can affect a principal's behaviour. To help meet this challenge, following are some suggestions to assist teachers with this responsibility.

Don't Project Negativity

Some teachers have problems with past principals and transfer their feelings to a new principal. This is simply projection. Teachers need to reflect on previous negative feelings and give new principals an opportunity to build effective learning relationships. If given a chance, principals might earn respect instead of hostility.

Expect Conflict

Everyone, including principals, is entitled to a few bad days. Principals are only human. If they boil over on a given day, it is wise to give them time to move beyond it. Teachers should try to not take things personally. They should focus on the problem and not on the person. Teachers can listen and learn. Chapter 9 will offer further useful ideas about conflict and disagreement.

Don't Turn Molehills into Mountains

Teachers should think about alternatives. A small gripe, when focused on obsessively, can get blown out of proportion and lead to a confrontation with a principal that hurts effective learning relationships. Teachers can make the choice to handle situations interpersonally and approach a principal as a unique, thinking, and emotional individual. If teachers have legitimate gripes, they should reflect about choices. Then they should share concerns. Principals don't know about concerns unless informed.

Think about Timing

If teachers have negative or positive comments to make, they should approach the principal at the right time. Principals can be very busy and under a lot of pressure on any given day. It is wise for teachers to wait it out. When the pressure is off, chances are good that a principal will give an opportunity to discuss the matter. If teachers insist on trying to talk at a bad time, principals can sense a power struggle and they have the power.

Don't Let Principals Intimidate You

Principals don't always act professionally. They are guilty of playing favorites and other forms of nonprofessional behavior. Teachers should not allow this to stop them from talking with the principal. Teachers are never happy shifting concerns, and principals seldom respect teachers who are afraid of them.

Don't Be Friends with Principals

A relationship with a principal is a professional relationship. It should be kept that way. The distance between teachers and principals is often a fine line. But the principal is the teacher's boss. When a teacher gets too personal, it almost always turns out badly. Stay interpersonal and don't be either too personal or too formal.

Clear the Air

When teachers make a mistake, a teacher's response can injure an effective learning relationship with the principal. Teachers should clean the slate with an open discussion. If a teacher has an issue with a principal and accepts part of the fault, the mature thing to do is "fess up" and move on.

Not All Principals Enjoy Their Roles

Some principals would prefer to be simply teachers again. But they can contribute more as a principal and they make a better income for their families. Teacher should view this as edifying. It gives insight into the role of principals and helps to understand them. Being a good principal is difficult. Sometimes principals who try the hardest to win the respect of teachers never fully succeed because of personality traits they cannot change. Teachers can try to understand and help a principal out.

Principals Can Be Mentors

A mentor is a person in a key position who takes a personal interest in a person's teaching and acts as an adviser. If a teacher builds the right relationship with a principal, the principal might counsel and guide over a period of time, even if no longer at the same school. Cate Coulacos Prato (2015) observes that a principal can offer a valuable mentoring experience.

Be Ethical

Appropriate ethical behavior on the part of both teachers and principals is essential to effective learning relationships. To maintain a teacher's side of the bargain, the following tips are presented:

- Maintain open and honest communication about ethical concerns. Tell the whole story regarding any problems that develop. Deception damages effective learning relationships.
- In the wake of ethical discussion, teachers should not discuss the principal in a negative way with other teachers. This is considered by many to be unethical. Teachers need not approve of everything a principal does, but sometimes it's best to keep attitudes to oneself.
- Try not to be influenced by either a principal or another teacher to perform unethical acts. A good way to take a stand on any questionable situation is to ask openly, "Is this ethical?"

CONCLUSION

Building and maintaining effective learning relationships with principals is a human relations challenge. It's not always easy. Yet it is an essential step in the teacher communication process. And it's a wise investment. Teachers may be used to one principal one day, only to discover that they have a different principal the next day. Knowing how to build effective learning relationships with principals is a communication challenge and a professional survival strategy.

EIGHT

Communicating and Conflict

> A peaceable classroom or school results when the values and skills of cooperation, communication, tolerance, positive emotional expression, and conflict resolution are taught and supported throughout the culture of school. —*Kathryn L. Girard*

Disagreement is nearly an everyday fare for teachers. Students, colleagues, and administrators supply plenty of sources for conflict. Conflict seems to be an inevitable part of teaching, and the need to manage conflict effectively is always with teachers. When conflict is viewed as inherently negative, it is treated as a weakness in a classroom or school—a flaw in design and operation. It is something to be avoided or eliminated as soon as possible. Peace and stability need to return in order for a classroom or school to be seen as "normal."

The view of conflict in this chapter is quite different. It emphasizes that interpersonal and organizational conflicts are not inherently negative or positive. They vary in terms of being productive or destructive. Conflicts can be relatively beneficial or harmful, depending on the attitudes and skills of a teacher. It is the way conflict is handled that is damaging or advantageous for a teacher.

This chapter helps teachers to effectively communicate through interpersonal or organizational conflict. Conflict is communication and can be handled through both command and relational communication. If teachers want to deal effectively with the conflict, they need effective communication attitudes and skills. Although all conflict is not rooted in poor communication, it always involves communication.

Dealing with interpersonal and organizational conflict requires information on three key areas: (1) Conflict and how it works, including its benefits. (2) The different types of conflict. (3) how teachers can handle it.

CONFLICT AS COMMUNICATION

An ERIC paper (Girard, 1996) examined the impact of relationship, task, and role conflict on teaching performance in schools. The paper looked at how teachers respond to conflict as related to interpersonal issues, personal taste, values, and lack of clarity toward work. It suggests that conflict is a topic of growing importance to teaching:

- Teachers spend significant time dealing with conflict.
- Conflict management is an increasingly important skill for teachers.
- Communication is the arena of conflict.

There are various causes of conflict. Among the causes are the following:

- Communication failure
- Personality clashes
- Value and goal differences
- Responsibility issues
- Competition for limited resources

Two important inferences can be drawn. One, conflict is a major part of teaching. Second, teachers need to get a handle on the complex dynamics of conflict. Conflict happens whenever teachers are involved in interdependent relationships. When teachers are interactive, many situations lead to conflict.

Handling conflict is about communicating effectively through conflict situations. When teachers know what conflict is and how it works, they can make some sense of it and its communication dynamics. They are better able to figure out what they can do. For example, a communication-oriented definition of conflict suggests productive ways for managing conflict.

One communication-oriented definition is offered by John Stewart (2007). He defines conflict as "verbally and nonverbally expressed disagreement between individuals or groups in an organization." Though broad, the definition points out some important ideas. It emphasizes that conflict is expressed with words or through nonverbal behaviors such as tone of voice or facial gestures. It concentrates on communication rather than on psychology, suggesting that conflict is not mostly about interpreting the motives of people. It's about communicating with people.

In addition, the definition sees conflict as a natural part of human organizations. People have disagreements. They are different. Conflict results from different points of views. People see and value things differently. They vary in beliefs about how things are and how they should be. The French philosopher Jean-Paul Sartre (1989) said, "Hell is other people." He may have understood the fundamental social nature of human conflict.

It's understandable why teachers look at conflict as a negative experience. It diverts their time and energy away from organizational and instructional tasks. It represents how polarized individuals and groups can be in schools. It obstructs cooperative action and decreases productivity. But a negative approach to conflict is the problem. Teachers need to begin seeing conflict as a positive and creative occurrence. Conflict has benefits.

THE BENEFITS OF CONFLICT

If conflict is natural—representing reality—then it cannot always be negative. Consequently, teachers who think about the negative part of conflict may need to "mutate their metaphors." They need to see conflict as beneficial to teacher communication. Conflict has the potential to:

- Open up hidden issues in relationships
- Clarify issues in discussions
- Improve the quality of individual and organizational problem-solving
- Increase participation in decision-making
- Increase understanding and cooperation

Conflicts can be valuable for teachers and schools. Conflict stimulates creative problem-solving, generates more effective ideas, and fine-tunes relationships. It provides opportunities to test ideas, demonstrate skills, understand other people, and develop trust. Most important, conflict can improve the quality of information and relationships.

Conflict Can Develop Effective Learning Relationships

There is a potential energy that conflict can bring to teacher relationships. It helps teachers learn something new about each other. For example, there is a heated debate in a school about where new computers should be located. Two teachers want them located in two different places, and an administrator is caught in between. The administrator could avoid the conflict by making an "executive decision" and ordering the computer to be put in one place or the other. Instead, she suggests a meeting to bring the teachers together. In the meeting, the teachers list alternative solutions. Funds could be raised to purchase portable carts for the computers or mobile laptops can be purchased. They could work out a schedule of when computers would be at a particular location. A workable solution is found. Most important, the two teachers realize that they didn't handle the conflict very well. They realize they could have initiated talk at the beginning. The conflict shows them that they are capable of talking reasonably with each other, and they become committed to "listen first, ask questions later" next time. They begin to develop a more effective learning relationship.

Conflict Can Improve Decision Making

The adversary system of judicial courts operates on the assumption that truth and justice emerge from the clash of ideas. Disagreements often lead to more workable decisions and relationships. Conflicts can lead to discussion and dialogue where teachers get to have their say and take part in decision making. If ideas are imposed upon them, teachers can feel disenfranchised and carry around resentments. This will affect future performance, cooperation, and decisions. A shared decision is not necessarily the best decision but it can build relationships and a sense of community. It gets the task done. Teachers are part of the decision and more likely to respect it.

Conflict Can Get Feelings Out

Handling conflict well is not about allowing people to scream at the wall or pound on a desk. Feelings must be communicated appropriately. But teachers need opportunities to express feelings productively. Conflict can be an opportunity for getting feelings out. If the energy of a feeling like anger can be channeled into positive discussions or dialogues, the feeling is used to find creative solutions and develop more effective relationships.

Conflicts Can Promote Confident Relationships

There is always uncertainty about what people will do when things get difficult. The first argument is a major event. But the confidence that follows is even more important. Successful conflict management helps relationships experience new confidence and security. Often relationships that avoid conflict are the most insecure and unproductive because they remain untested. Relationships are tested by conflict. Confidence develops by communicating successfully through conflict.

TYPES OF CONFLICT

Conflict is pervasive in organizations, including schools. It is a part of what makes us human. All humans are different, and conflict reflects the human condition. To avoid conflict means avoiding differences. Without differences, humans lose their humanity.

To communicate effectively through conflict, teachers need to recognize that not all conflict is the same. The goal is to identify the type of conflict. Depending on what a conflict is about, it must be handled differently. There are three basic types of conflict: conflict over content, conflict over roles, and conflict over values.

Conflict Over Content

Conflict can reflect differing views about content. It can involve disagreements over fact or meaning. People can disagree with the fact that Columbus landed in the Western Hemisphere in 1492, and that can be confirmed or disconfirmed. Or they can disagree about whether he "discovered" America at all, and that is a matter of meaning and interpretation. The most important question for teachers is about the content of the conflict—is it about fact or meaning? A labor contract can say that a teacher is entitled to an office, but what does "office" mean? Is an office a separate work space or part of a room divided into sections?

Conflict Over Roles

Conflict can also reflect differing views about roles. For example, conflict happens in families, the basic human organization. Parents look forward to when their children become independent adults but then continue to see their children as "little boys" or "little girls" long after the kids enter adolescence. Consequently, conflict begins to happen in the family. Parents won't let go, and the kids move too fast. Squabbles about little things like coming home at dusk increase. But what is the conflict really about? If the disagreement is seen as about facts, a lot of time may be spent arguing that kids still need to take out the garbage. But if parents recognize that the disagreement is about roles, then they can talk about identities and maybe work something out. They can compromise with intermediate roles—giving increased but limited responsibilities and freedoms.

Teachers need to see why social labels become so important to students and are often a source of conflict. Whether it be "gay," "African American," "Hispanic," "Asian," "person," or "Native American," social labels reveal disagreement over fundamental identities. Social labels are responses to questions with consequences: Who has authority? Who has the power to define people?

Conflict Over Values

Conflict can also reflect differing views about values. Researchers recognize that schools are cultures. Schools develop cultural values that strongly affect the way teachers and students view a school's primary purposes. Cultural values cannot be simply imposed. They develop over time and involve disagreements over such values as expectations of staff and students. But conflict over cultural values is necessary. Well-defined and clarified values are better than ambiguity. Schools, whether traditional or progressive, perform better if all participants—teachers, students, administrators, and parents—are on the same page about values. Conflict about values is most effectively dealt with in a structured way where there is an opportunity for mutual respect, learning, and supporting relationships.

HOW NOT TO COMMUNICATE THROUGH CONFLICT

Teachers need to keep in mind that effective conflict management knows the difference between reacting and responding. Reacting is reflexive in nature. On the other hand, responding is reflective. Responses involve thinking and choices. The following ways of communicating through conflict are reactive. Reactive approaches do not appreciate that whenever teachers are involved in conflict, there are four elements to the communication process: the teacher, the other person, the subject, and the climate. Figure 8.1 illustrates a circle where each element makes up one quarter of conflict. In order to respond to conflict, teacher communication must include every element.

Three of the elements of conflict are easy to understand. The teacher and the other person are the conflict participants. They could be a teacher and a student, parent, or administrator. The subject, of course, is the topic of the conflict. On the other hand, the last element needs explanation. The climate of conflict includes the physical and emotional environments. The physical environment can be the communication mode (cell phone, face-to-face) and the physical condition (like room temperature or proxemics). The emotional environment can include the moods of the participants and the emotive power of the topic. For example, talking about abortion rights tends to be more controversial than discussing the three branches of the federal government.

When teachers react to conflict, they ignore or cancel out one or more of the elements. According to Virginia Satir, there are four reactive or ineffective ways of communicating through conflict: placating, pouncing, distracting, and computing.

Placating Ignores One's Self

Some people believe that it is "better to keep the peace than to fight" or "relationship can't stand a fight." Both are not necessarily true. When a teacher asks a student, "What's wrong?" and the student responds, "It's not important," what the student is saying is, "I'm not important." That's placating. Placating denies the importance of one's self. Placators fail to acknowledge their own point of view. They avoid conflict and eliminate themselves by using statements that end the conversation before it starts.

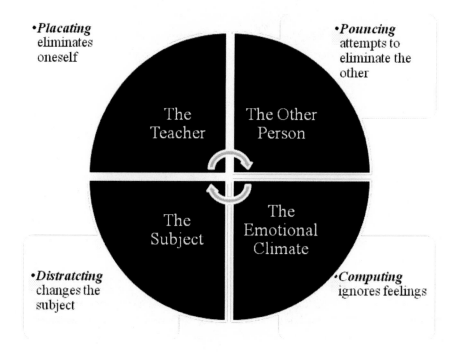

Figure 8.1. Four Elements of Conflict

When people placate in a conflict, they don't express feelings, thoughts, and wishes. They may communicate indirectly by frowning, crying, or whispering something under their breath. They subordinate their needs to the needs of others. Nonverbal behaviors include backing up, looking down, and other subordinate postures.

Pouncing Ignores Others

Some people try to drive away others in conflict by pouncing. They "jump on others" and blame them for disagreements. The goal is to eliminate other people. Pouncing is based on the belief that "my view is the only right view." Pouncing includes name calling, rejecting, hostile questioning, sarcastic joking, accusing, blaming, and threatening that demand the other person change.

When a student in a work group asks another group member, "What's wrong with my work?" a pouncer responds, "It's not good work." There's no attempt to compromise. What the pouncer means is, "You are not important." That's pouncing. Pouncing is attempting to control a conflict. It is unresponsive because it fails to acknowledge other people's opinions and feelings. When people pounce, they communicate an air of superiority and intimidation. They run the gamut from deadly quiet to loud sarcasm. They point fingers or make fists. Pouncers are intent on being right and don't really listen to what other people are saying, even when asked a direct question.

Distracting Changes the Subject

Some people assume that if the subject is changed, the conflict goes away. It doesn't. The clearest sign of distracting in a conflict is an abrupt change of the topic. When an administrator says, "We need to talk about our disagreement today," and a teacher responds, "I have a lot of papers to read today," what the distractor means is, "I'm not comfortable talking about the conflict. Let's avoid it." That's distracting. Distracting is diverting a conflict. It is unresponsive because it fails to acknowledge the subject of the conflict.

Computing Ignores Emotions

Some people believe that "grown people don't get emotional." But grown people do get emotional. Feelings always accompany thought. One challenge in a conflict is to deal with emotions rather than ignore them. When a teacher ignores the emotions of a parent during a difficult conference and says, "Let's remain professional," what the computer means is, "I'm not comfortable with feelings." That's computing. Computing dehumanizes conflict. It is unresponsive because it fails to acknowledge another person's feelings. When people compute, they remain impersonal. They use abstract and technical language. They only want to deal with "the cold, hard facts." Computers are detached and often talk in the third person. They remain expressionless as long as possible.

CONCLUSION

The most effective way for teachers to communicate through conflict is by responding. Responding shows thoughtfulness and an appreciation for relational communication. It tends to all four elements of the conflict: the teacher, the other person, the subject, and the climate. Responding involves paying attention to feelings, and it "stands up for its own rights." It asks about the other person's feelings and attitudes. It's comfortable with feelings and "sticks to the topic."

This chapter concludes with suggestions by Alan Sillar et al. (1982). Using certain kinds of statements constitute acts of responding. According to Sillars, responding to conflict involves the following:

- Using descriptive language—make nonevaluative statements about events and behaviors related to the conflict. Be descriptive, not prescriptive. Describe behaviors and don't make judgments about character.
- Setting limits—use statements that qualify the nature and extent of the conflict. Don't expand a content conflict into an identity conflict unless it is already one.
- Practicing disclosure—share statements about mental and emotional information related to the conflict that the other person cannot observe such as thoughts about feelings, intentions, motivations, and history.
- Asking for genuine disclosure—solicit information from the other person about mental and emotional information related to the conflict that cannot be observed, even complaints about oneself.
- Offering support—make statements that express understanding, acceptance, and positive regard for the other person. Show empathy for what the other person experiences. Express appreciation for positive characteristics.
- Emphasizing commonalities—use statements that highlight common ground. Identify areas of agreement. List strengths before moving on to things that need improvement. This builds a positive foundation.
- Accepting responsibility—accept responsibility for conflicts for oneself or for all parties. Apologies help.
- Initiating problem-solving—initiate mutual consideration of alternatives and solutions.
- Using relationship reminders—remind others that the conflict exists within a broader context of mutual respect and relationship. Reminding a colleague about an event attended together also reminds him or her about a long-term relationship. Be careful to not distract, though.
- Reversing roles—take a couple minutes to think about the other person's point of view.
- Fractionating—break conflicts down into smaller pieces. This is good analysis and takes issues one at a time. It doesn't overwhelm some people.
- Avoiding "triggers"—triggers inflame conflicts. They can be the "last straw." Avoid using words, ideas, and judgments that will unnecessarily upset the other person. Sometimes it's better to describe a behavior than use a label. Calling a colleague irresponsible will not go down as well as observing that he or she is late for a meeting quite a bit.
- Avoiding "gunny sacking"—don't use a conflict as an opportunity to bring up all the bruises collected and nursed for days, weeks, or even years. Don't empty the sack all at once.

- Defusing conflict—reduce the energy level of conflict by listening, identifying areas of agreement, and maintaining nonverbal cadence. Move to a better location without an audience or with less distractions. Respond to and express feelings. Wait until a good time to talk about the conflict.

III

Teaching and Classroom
Communication

Part III looks at some challenging situations teachers face in classroom communication—dealing with teams and groups, making presentations, and communicating online—and helps teachers choose appropriate communication strategies. It's a starting point for thinking about issues found in today's classroom. The main idea is that classroom communication is a rhetorical situation. Teachers require rhetorical sensitivity to respond rather than react to classroom communication challenges.

RHETORICAL SITUATIONS

Communication theorist Lloyd Bitzer (1968) coined the phrase *rhetorical situation*. Rhetoric is purposeful communication that takes place in various settings. It is usually associated with persuasion. For example, Aristotle saw rhetoric as using all the available means of persuasion, so traditional views of rhetoric use emotion and information to change people's minds. Language has a persuasive or impressive effect on audience. Unfortunately, today rhetoric also implies a lack of sincerity or meaningful content.

Bitzer describes rhetoric as a situation or setting that has three characteristics: (1) a *challenge*, problem, or obstacle; (2) an *audience* open to changing views and helping implement changes; and (3) *constraints* that limit the range of available communication strategies and restrict a speaker's ability to affect the situation and change minds. Constraints include beliefs, attitudes, human relations skills, and authority. The three characteristics combine to form the context for communication choices. In addition, Bitzer's rhetorical situation is communicative. It downplays the command elements like persuasion, and it highlights relational elements like the role of communication styles.

Rhetorical Sensitivity

Rod Hart and Don Burks (1972) introduced the concept of *rhetorical sensitivity*. They argued that leadership, communication, and relationships are enhanced when people are "rhetorically sensitive" and communicate to reflect a particular situation or setting. One way to explain the concept is to compare a rhetorical sensitive communication style with two other types identified by Hart and Burks: *noble selves* and *rhetorical reflectors*.

Like all individuals, teachers have a predominant manner or communication style. Hart and Burks contrast the three general communication styles. *Noble selves* are people who perceive that they should not adapt to other people or to situations in any way that violates their beliefs, values, or normal activities. Noble selves stick to their personal ideals without variation and without adjusting to others. On the other extreme, *rhetorical reflectors* are people who communicate as if they have no beliefs, values, or normal actions to call their own. They present a different image to every person and situation. Rhetorical reflectors mold themselves to others' wishes with no personal scruples to follow.

In contrast to both extremes of the continuum, *rhetorical sensitives* show concern for self, others, and different situations. Rhetorical sensitives are people who accept human complexity and understand that individuals are composites of many selves. They attempt to balance self-interests with the interests of others. Rhetorical sensitives moderate the extremes of noble selves and rhetorical reflectors because they do the following:

- Take on a variety of roles.
- Avoid rigid patterns of communication.
- Respect the needs of other people but do not sacrifice their own ideas and feelings to placate others.
- Appreciate that ideas and feelings should be expressed only when it is appropriate to do so.
- Search for the best way to communicate ideas and feelings.

Teachers who are rhetorical sensitives appreciate that every communication message—oral or written—is polysemous. It has different possible meanings. As explained earlier, communication messages have meaning at the content or command level. They also have meanings at the emotional and relational levels. In schools, calm rationality is often valued and emotion is denigrated. Emotional displays are suppressed. But teachers can accurately understand messages only if they are able to recognize underlying meaning. Those messages always say something about a speaker's relationship with the listener, with other people and with the school itself.

Rhetorical sensitive teachers understand that "hidden rules" of communication are revealed by the timing of messages, by the audience selected or avoided, and by the argument proposed or suppressed. Without this understanding, teachers cannot produce the kinds of motivational effects they want or effectively interpret the information of others. For example, when a seasoned teacher tells a new teacher, "That's a pretty good idea, for a rookie," the message can mean a variety of things. It can be focused on the information (it is a good idea). It can be focused on emotion (the older teacher's pride in his or her guidance). Or it can be focused on the relationship (to firmly establish that the new teacher is a subordinate).

Rhetorical sensitivity helps teachers to listen for the relational implications of messages. Two kinds of implications are present in almost all messages. The first is the function of the message. Some messages are decision-making messages. They call for responses that focus on the problem. Responses that express disagreement are appropriate if objective and problem-oriented. Other messages can seem like decision-making messages but aren't. They might be ritualistic. For example, "What can we ever do to replace Alice?" does not really call for making a decision. The response, "Well, Fred could easily do quite well," can be inappropriate and might reveal important relational information.

The second implication is about the negotiation of roles. Often messages are invitations to affirm and accept roles in the structure of an organization. Teachers who do not understand this might respond in ways that challenge the hierarchy of the school or the authority of a person. Whoever said that the pen is mightier than the sword definitely knew what they were talking about. To humans, words are more than a means of communication; they shape roles, behaviors, feelings, and ultimately actions. Although swords can coerce us, nothing is more powerful than communication to shape who we are and who we are not. For example, teachers need to maintain their role as a school member. This requires some maintenance strategies. But some strategies work against negotiating a productive role. Avoidance behavior is a poor negotiating tool and can send the message that one does not affirm or accept one's role as a team member in a school.

In summary, rhetorical sensitivity is developed when teachers accept a number of relatively simple attitudes about communication:

- There are multiple levels of meaning.
- Effective communication requires demanding practice.
- Other teachers and students have something worthwhile to say.
- Physical (phone calls) and psychological (biases) distractions affect communication.

COMMUNICATION AND CLASSROOM CHANGE

Teachers are often placed in challenging classroom situations that trigger reactions instead of responses. The ability to deal with difficult classroom situations depends on the depth of a teacher's repertoire of attitudes and skills — the teacher's communication competence. The level of knowledge and adeptness either gives a teacher a wide range of strategies or reduces available choices. A full repertoire allows a teacher to see possibilities and constraints otherwise overlooked.

Successful and rhetorical sensitive teachers are able to deal with complicated situations because of their reserve of effective communication and human relations skills. They have the means to address situational factors that limit their freedom to choose. They have the competence to see how schools and classrooms are matrices of rhetorical situations, challenges, possibilities, and constraints.

One example is the challenge of communicating effectively through the process of change that is taking place in today's classroom. The changes require that teachers have smarter communication skills. Curricular reform, standardized testing, and alterations in teacher–student relationships create the need for *communication intelligence*. Traditional teachers were expected to use lecture and tests — one-way communication between the teacher and students. This approach depended mainly on authority. Expectations are changing and so must the approach of teachers. Teachers need to move beyond the role of simply being conduits of information and depend more on relationships. Information is now readily available on the Internet. Teachers are called on to be open to change and adaptation. This poses challenges for teachers who do not yet have the communication reasoning necessary for the new teaching and learning environment.

Improved teacher performance and effectiveness rely on how teachers respond to classroom change. According to change expert Gordon Lippitt (1969), teachers, like other people, tend to respond to unplanned and poorly planned changes in certain ways, like the following:

- Disbelief — disequilibrium and sense of unreality about change
- Projection — blaming someone else for the challenges
- Rationalization — trying to make sense of the change
- Acceptance — resignation (or, the new state of affairs is accepted)

Such reactions are understandable considering how changes increase uncertainty. There is uncertainty about teacher responsibilities and the nature of teacher–student relations. The most effective way teachers can respond intelligently to classroom change is by becoming learners and taking responsibility for their communication. This requires new information about the complexities of classroom communication. But information is not enough. Teachers need to be mindful that there will be contradictions between existing and new communication ideas.

A state of dissonance about contradictions within change must also be dealt with. For example, as teachers confront the need for more interpersonal relationships in the classroom, they also confront the reality that educational technology in some important ways can separate people. Texting can replace face-to-face and even phone conversations. Technology can come at the cost of interpersonal interactions. It has the potential for more impersonal contacts. Consequently, technology can create mental and emotional dissonance.

Dissonance is most effectively reduced through integrating contradictions by moving away from black and white, right and wrong, and dualistic thinking. All change is two-fold. It has its advantages and disadvantages. It has its command and relational communication issues. Consequently, the most effective way to communicate through change is to recognize that responsive teacher communication requires the successful integration of communication's command and relational elements. Technology has the capacity to increase a sense of loneliness and impersonal communication, but teachers can focus intentionally on its equal potential to enhance connections and interpersonal relationships.

Guidelines for Responding to Classroom Change

Teachers who want to respond to classroom change need rhetorical sensitivity and communication intelligence. If the goal is to open up to change and overcome dissonance about it, three guidelines are suggested:

Engage in dialogue.

Dissonance about change will be less intense when teachers understand why change is happening and what the advantages are for change. Dialogue about classroom change can do this most effectively. Dialogue can help teachers to understand the when, what, where, and why of classroom change. Discussions ease fears and dissonance about change. Dialogue stimulates many good ideas and educates teachers about potential communication problems that might arise when changes are implemented in classrooms. Dialogue can increase a teacher's rhetorical sensitivity and communication IQ. Mistrust about change arises when teachers have inadequate information. They feel lost and do not know how to influence the process. Dialogue helps teachers feel connected to other teachers and respond productively to classroom changes

Search for information.

When teachers are kept in self-imposed darkness or get incomplete information, rumors and insecurity start to circulate. This creates dissonance. Rumors can have an enormous influence on teachers and their responses to change. But teachers can counter rumors and become increasingly more secure about changes. Personal research empowers teachers and prevents them from feeling helpless. Teachers can learn the whole story and come to know where they stand. Teachers need to know how a contemplated change will affect teacher–student relationships, increase classroom conflicts, or violate previous classroom norms. Dissonance affects a teacher's willingness to accept change. Accurate information can reduce dissonance and help teachers to visualize the rewards of new attitudes and behaviors.

Communicate feelings.

Responses to change are more easily integrated when teachers communicate feelings, blow off steam, or connect with others. An informal "gripe session" can give teachers useful feedback about the pros and cons of change. Change is inevitable and unavoidable. It scares teachers because it takes away the familiar and introduces the unknown. Fear, uncertainty, and dissonance can be the hallmarks of change. But expressing feelings is a positive component of teacher communication that helps teachers to take ownership of feelings. It prevents feelings from controlling behavior and allows teachers to collectively shape emotions and attitudes for more constructive purposes.

CONCLUSION

Part III helps teachers to increase competence and rhetorical sensitivity by suggesting ways to deal with a variety of classroom situations. Chapter 9 offers suggestions about effective group or team communication. Chapter 10 discusses ideas that help teachers make effective classroom presentations. Chapter 11 presents a hybrid teaching method that combines lecturing and discussing—the instructional discussion. Finally, chapter 12 emphasizes the attitudes and skills needed to communicate effectively with new technology.

NINE

Group and Team Communication

Researchers report that, regardless of the subject matter, students working in small groups tend to learn more of what is taught and retain it longer than when the same content is presented in other instructional formats. —*Barbara Gross Davis*

Part II looked at the various issues that teachers find when attempting to develop effective learning relationships with parents and principals. It recognized issues of diversity, sex, and age. It integrated the concepts of effective learning relationships, communities of practice, dialogue, and the fusion of horizons as ways of building productive communication among teachers, students, parents, and principals. This chapter focuses on how these issues apply to teachers and students as members of groups or teams.

In the typical school, the principal is at the top of the pyramid. Often he or she manages or controls the operation of the school, assumes responsibility for outcomes, and, it is hoped, involves teachers in decision-making. With the team concept, the principal operates within the team itself. He or she takes time to involve teachers in creating goals, delegating responsibilities, communicating information, and directing themselves. The performance of a team depends on building effective learning relationships and communities of practice all team members make contributions. The motivation to perform comes from other team members. Consequently, it is a way for individuals to communicate together. Good team members help other members to understand and are willing to enter dialogue.

A DEFINITION OF A TEAM

A team is a collection of individuals who share a unifying task or goal. Teams are groups of people with different skills and subtasks who work together on a common project or goal. Teams mesh functions and encourage mutual support. Teams teach individuals to pool knowledge, tackle problems, take on responsibilities, share perspectives, develop social support, resolve conflict, and create shared identities.

Benefits of Teamwork

The team concept in education is more popular today than ever before. Entire books have been written on the subject. Educators across the country offer team-building workshops. Many schools districts are retraining superintendents, principals, and teachers to become team leaders. There is evidence that educational work teams often achieve greater productivity than traditional approaches.

Group work helps students develop a host of social and cognitive skills, including problem-solving and decision-making abilities. Ellen Sarkisian (2010) recognizes that positive team experiences open up students to sharing ideas for constructive criticism and comparison. Properly structured groups reinforce skills in time management, discussion, giving and receiving feedback, accepting challenges, and communication.

The benefit for teachers is also clear. Teachers can assign more complex, authentic problems to teams of students than they can to individuals. Group work introduces more creativity in teaching. Teams approach tasks and solve problems in novel ways. Group assignments are also useful when a limited number of viable project topics are distributed among students. In addition, they reduce the number of final products for instructors to grade.

Whatever the benefits, effective teachers assign group work that fulfills learning objectives of the course and encourages cooperation. Teachers are aware that group projects can add work for them at different points in the process and introduce grading complexities such as how to evaluate group and individual performances.

CHARACTERISTICS OF EFFECTIVE TEAMS

There are common characteristics of effective teams. The purpose, goal, or main objective is known and understood by all members. There is open, direct, and honest communication. Someone takes leadership responsibilities, or leadership is shared on a contingent basis. There are regular reviews of what needs to be done and how well things have gone. The team has access to adequate resources and members know how to get those resources. Most important, a productive team develops effective learning relationships and a community of practice that emphasize the group as greater than the sum of its parts. In addition, effective team members need certain characteristics.

Effective Team Members

The ability to work well with others is not only an important teaching skill but a skill for teachers to pass on to students. As potential team members, students should learn some things ahead of time in order to be effective. Effective group members accept and promote the *Four Cs of team membership*:

- Willingness to *communicate*
- Willingness to *critically think*
- Willingness to *creatively think*
- Willingness to *collaborate*

The Four Cs show how team members need to manage their behavior so that all actions are in the best interest of the group as a whole. John Larmer (2013) suggests that this is best accomplished with effective communication. Effective team communication happens through effective learning relationships and dialogue. Both promote an exchange of ideas and provide vehicles for engaging and transformative thinking. Both encourage interpersonal and intrapersonal competence that emerges between persons. Team communication happens between people about a subject matter or task at hand.

Teams do not primarily focus on the individual acquisition of information but on members thinking critically and creatively. Members engage with each other's ideas, testing those ideas against others and recognizing productive from nonproductive ones. Consequently, effective team members are willing to collaborate. Like effective learning relationships, teamwork is not simply a technique for teachers to transmit knowledge but a way for students to construct meaning together. The ultimate goal is to create a community of practice.

Effective team members are sensitive to the needs of others, supporting and helping to promote effective learning relationships in which everyone wants to contribute. Team members accept the roles of others and offer constructive feedback when mistakes are made. They do not simply complain about past mistakes; that is not constructive and does little to improve performance. Shared values must be clarified and developed. Before working through differences, team members must identify areas of agreement and build a positive foundation.

Finally, effective team members approach all topics or tasks as possibly suitable for the group approach. Each objective is studied to determine how a team approach will produce the best results. If one simply requires a "right" answer, it may need less time for group work. When a project needs the special knowledge, experience, or skills of different students, it requires the team approach. Team members ask questions like: Where does a task fit into the overall group objective? Is the group objective specific and workable? Do team members have the right mix of characteristics?

Clearly, the effectiveness of a team member depends on attitudes toward the group. All teams are different, but no team functions effectively if even one member has a negative attitude. Regardless of a team's composition and leadership, certain attitudes must be present among group members to help develop effective learning relationships and a community of practice. Individuals need to do the following:

- Accept group work and self-direction, and work for the team as a whole. All team members need to be invested in the values of the activity.
- Practice the Four Cs of team membership (communicate, critical thinking, creative thinking, and collaboration). Members achieve more for the group if everyone acts as independent thinkers.
- Take responsibility for self-discipline. Teams that develop a community of practice create less hierarchical styles than traditional groups.
- Respect that contributions from other team members will be diverse and reflect a blend of talent and abilities that give group work power.
- Maintain openness to prejudices of all team members, regardless of cultural, ethnic, and racial differences.

Roles of Team Members

Team members play a variety of roles in groups, both productive and destructive. Some roles are functional because they encourage effective learning relationships, accomplish a group's objective through systematic problem-solving (task), and help interpersonal relations of the group (process). Examples of functional group roles include the following:

- Gatekeepers—members who praise, agree with, and accept the ideas of others in the group by encouraging the participation of others
- Harmonizers—members who mediate group conflicts and relieve tension by creating a safe environment for participation
- Standard Setters—members who raise questions about goals and express standards for the group and assess movement toward goals
- Humanizers—members who show an interest in human relations and encourage expression of feelings

Some team roles are dysfunctional. They hinder effective learning relationships, systematic problem-solving, and the accomplishments of group objectives. They include the following:

- Placators—members who treat the communication as closed by withholding input and denying their own point of view. They are insecure and less motivated to accomplish tasks. They serve as friendly followers and go along passively.
- Pouncers—members who intimidate other group members, especially placators, into submission. They like to give orders and force others to agree with them. They also deflate and antagonize others.
- Distractors—members who dwell on unimportant issues and nonessential considerations. They use the group to get personal attention or sympathy. Distractors direct groups away from goals and toward individual concerns.
- Computers—members who show no interest in human relations and are extremely task-oriented. They want to finish the task even at the expense of others' input, feelings, and social interaction. This leads a group to make decisions not shared by all members and guarantees poor performance.

TEAM DEVELOPMENT STAGES

Teachers can't expect new teams to perform well when students first come together. Creating an effective team takes time. Members need to experience the stages of team development—changing from a collection of strangers to a united group with common values and goals. Bruce Tuckman's forming, storming, norming, and performing model describes the stages of team development. It helps new teams become effective more quickly. Tuckman (1965) came up with the memorable phrase "forming, storming, norming, and performing" and used it to describe the path that most teams follow on their way to high performance.

Forming

In the *forming* stage, team members are anxious because they don't fully understand what the goal of the group is or what work the team will do. The tendency is for someone to take on a dominant role at this stage. Roles and responsibilities are unclear. Consequently, some people become task-oriented. To relieve tension, they quickly move to the task and ignore social development.

During the forming stage, students need to make an effort to get to know each other. Like in a community of practice, team members need to be welcomed to participate and belong to the group. This is when members either become invested in the values and activities of the group or not. If movement to the task is too quick, team members do not get a sense of belonging to the group. Consequently, they become passive and allow others to make decisions. This results in alienation and even resentment. Teams that don't pay attention to the social needs of forming often do most of the work. But they run the risk of being "hung out to dry" by less involved members when the group performs the task.

Storming

Following forming, a team moves into the *storming* phase. This is where team members start to push against the boundaries (tasks, role, and responsibilities) established in the forming stage. This is the stage where many teams fail. Storming starts when there is a conflict of personalities, styles, or roles. Students work in different ways for all sorts of reasons, but if differing styles cause unforeseen problems, they become frustrating. Team members challenge authority and jockey for position to clarify roles.

If team responsibilities have not been defined collectively, members can feel uncomfortable with the decision-making approach. They can question the value of the team's goal and resist taking part in the process. Team members who simply stick with the task at hand experience stress, as they didn't work to develop effective learning relationships with other team members. The crucial point for the storming stage is for team members to openly and honestly discuss the conflict. If teams do not openly discuss the conflict, the conflict will dominate the team. Without addressing conflict, a group cannot norm. If a group cannot *norm*, it cannot perform.

Groups can address and resolve conflict in a number of ways. Team members can vote. They can rearrange roles. They can adjust responsibilities. They can revise group objectives and goals. However the means, it is important that teams approach the storming phase head-on and move on to the norming stage.

Norming

If a team successfully weathers the storming phase, it can move on to the *norming* stage. Norming is when team members downplay differences, appreciate similarities, recognize other members' strengths, and authentically join a community of practice. Team members know each other well, may even socialize, are able to ask one another for help, and provide constructive feedback. Members develop a stronger commitment to team values, roles, relationships, and goals. They practice effective learning relationships. Communication moves to dialogue, whereby members are willing to share prejudices and to fuse horizons. Teachers should keep in mind that there is often a prolonged overlap between storming and norming. As new issues come up, teams may relapse to the storming stage.

Performing

When a team has taken the time and effort to create a community of practice, it reaches the *performing* stage. The structures and processes that the group has set up support successful performing. Work is delegated and members continue to develop effective learning relationships. It feels easy to be part of a team at this stage. Members have no motivation to disrupt performance. Teams that reach this stage perform well. Team members may even find it challenging as relationships end.

CONCLUSION

The aim of effective team members is to help other members perform well. To do this, team members must do the right thing at the right time. First, members can identify the stage of team development and be aware of the team's needs at each stage. Second, members can consider what they need to do to help the team start off right and form a productive group. Third, members can help other members understand their roles, help them understand how they can move the team forward, and adjust behaviors and communication appropriately. If a team has a sense of belonging and group members form attachments—effective learning relationships—they develop a community of practice. This allows team members to feel at ease and trust each other.

Effective learning relationships and a community of practice encourage dialogue and the fusion of horizons. Group members become invested in a team that has a culture of participation and belonging. Teams that develop a community of practice allow the group and individuals to achieve common goals.

TEN

Effective Teacher Presentations

> If you are simply teaching content, a machine will fast replace you. [Twenty-first-century] education is far more than the content. It is about preparing students for an ever-changing world. —*Karen Boyes*

Part III introduced the concept of rhetorical situations. If teachers want to understand the full dynamics of effective oral presentations, they need to take into account the rhetorical situation of the presentation—the teaching context, the student audience, and the emotional climate. Consequently, this chapter looks at how effective presentations require analyzing the rhetorical situation, developing an appropriate learning objective, organizing the presentational structure, and presenting information in a way that captures students' attention and engages their thinking.

ANALYZING THE RHETORICAL SITUATION

As described earlier, traditional rhetoric is purposeful communication that takes place in various situations and is usually associated with persuasion. It uses all the available means of persuasion. In this regard, rhetoric is a tool that uses emotion and information to change people's minds. In response, Bitzer (1968) redefines rhetoric as a "situation" that includes the characteristics of a challenge, an audience capable of having minds changed, and constraints that restrict a speaker's ability to affect the situation and change minds. These characteristics combine to form the emotional climate within which teaching presentations are developed.

Bitzer's approach suggests that teachers need a *communicative IQ* that downplays persuasion and focuses on the relational aspect of presentations. The first step for teachers is to analyze the teaching context, the student audience, and the emotional climate.

The Teaching Context

The context of teaching includes various factors—cognitive, physical, social, and personal—that influence the oral presentation. For example, the cognitive factor often requires teachers to rethink the purpose of the presentation. From one perspective, the goal of teaching is to help students make choices, not persuade them to do one thing or the other. Of course, teaching always has a level of persuasion. At the very least, teachers want to persuade students to learn and think. This can be called "soft" persuasion. It is not "hard" in the sense that it uses all available means to convince others of specific ways of thinking and acting. With soft persuasion, teaching allows students to think for themselves.

The social factor of teaching is not about supplying information but about involving students in learning. The philosopher Martin Heidegger (1968) believed that teaching is more challenging than learning exactly because it "lets learning happen." The challenge is not for teachers to have a larger store of knowledge but to teach nothing else but learning itself. The model of apprenticeship emphasizes letting learning happen and the relatedness of teacher to student. The teacher is ahead of the apprentice in learning alone and continues to learn. A teacher's expertise is not in holding static knowledge but in a growing "teachability." According to the apprenticeship model, the purpose of teaching is to model the proper relatedness of a learner to a subject.

In other words, soft persuasion involves teachers educating, not pontificating. In this teaching context, the challenge is not to think of teaching as being an expert in one's field of knowledge but to think of it as letting learning occur. Ultimately, promoting effective learning relationships, a community of practice, and dialogue work towards this goal.

The physical environment is a second factor in the teaching context— the classroom. The challenge for teachers is to set up a beneficial physical environment for student learning. The possible constraints include student seating arrangements, lighting, heat, time of day, and even the day of the week. For instance, the arrangement of the desks encourages certain kinds of interactions and discourages others. If a teacher wants to include breaks in a lecture where student "buzz groups" discuss an issue before returning to the presentation, then arranging desks for student groups is appropriate. But the arrangement is counterproductive if it encourages side conversations and interferes with students giving full attention.

A third factor of the teaching context is the social environment. The challenge is reinforcing the relationship between teacher and students. Relationship plays a significant role in a successful presentation. The immediacy or approachability of the teacher influences how students respond and the kind of questions they ask. Consequently, if a teacher is interested in developing effective learning relationships with students and helping them experience a sense of belonging in a community of practice, an interpersonal approach is essential. A presentation is not solely about content; it is also constrained by the need for peoplemaking. Every presentation should send the message that students are unique, thinking, and emotional human beings.

Finally, personal context is a fourth factor. The challenge is about what a teacher brings to the classroom. For example, one possible constraint is the stress a teacher may be taking into class. At one level, teaching is performance, and "the show must go on." A teacher must enter the classroom without emotionally contaminating it. But it is useful for teachers to remind themselves that they are human and assess emotions before class. This gives them the opportunity to readjust emotional states and prepare for professional responsibilities.

Personal context constraints also include teachers' attitudes about learning, teaching, students, and the topic. Teachers who believe students can learn the content and communicate that belief to students encourage success in the same way that teachers who do not believe that students can learn encourage failure. Teachers "teach" who they are. To give effective oral presentations, teachers must believe in themselves, in students, and in the subject.

The Student Audience

Knowing the student audience is important for an oral presentation because it partly determines the content of the presentation. The content should vary depending on the background and experience of the student audience. In other words, a focused topic is important, but keeping a specific audience in mind is equally important. Let's imagine a coach giving a presentation on important practice techniques for becoming a better tennis player. If the coach's audience is beginning players, or students who know little about the game, the techniques need to be different than if the coach is presenting to students who have enough experience to consider entering tournaments. For beginning students, the steps would be basic, but with more experienced students, the steps would be advanced. Although the topic of the presentations would be the same, the information would be different.

The same is true of oral presentations where teachers want students to change attitudes and behaviors. When presenting information about possible changes, teachers need to identify the level of change and the students who may be inclined to pursue the change. For example, a presentation about developing active listening skills has different audiences. One audience includes introverted students who are reticent to speak in class. In this case, explaining how change will benefit them by increasing involvement in class discussions might be a useful strategy. Another audience includes extroverted students who tend to dominate conversations. In this case, a social constructionist argument about the benefits of letting others speak may be important points to address.

Knowing the intended audience for a presentation answers other questions that frequently arise. For instance, teachers wonder when the use of jargon (words or language related to a specific field) or acronyms (abbreviations of longer names/terms) is appropriate. If an audience has previous experience with the terms, then they don't need to be explained. For example, if a teacher is giving a presentation to students with numerous classroom experiences and observations, educational jargon can and should be used. But if an audience includes beginning education students, terms need to be explained or not used at all.

The Emotional Climate

The objectives of oral presentations cannot be met unless teachers provide students with a socially and emotionally healthy classroom environment. This claim is supported by arguments made throughout this book and by evidence that emotionally supportive classrooms are related to greater student motivation, interest, enjoyment, and engagement. The quality of social and emotional interactions in a classroom—among students and teachers—creates the emotional climate. The emotional climate includes characteristics such as teacher sensitivity to student needs; warm, friendly, respectful, and immediate teaching behaviors; and teacher regard for students' perspectives and encouragement of active participation.

Students' relationships with supportive teachers promote a sense of connectedness and community in the classroom that helps to develop effective learning relationships. Student reports of healthy relationships with teachers are positively linked to engagement in a learning community. In contrast, students who experience inadequate relationships with teachers often feel disconnected or alienated and are more likely to disengage.

In addition, the nature of the topic of the presentation is an important factor in the emotional climate of the classroom and presentation. Many topics are unpleasant or controversial. Teachers should not avoid those issues. For example, teachers cannot present the history of the American education without discussing slavery, Jim Crow, and racism, topics that can make students uncomfortable. But without an understanding of slavery and segregation, American history makes no sense. Learning about controversial issues helps students become informed and active thinkers—seeing the importance of voting, supporting basic democratic values, and influencing educational policy.

Engaging students in oral presentations is necessary for the development of critical thinking in students. To include thoughtful, productive, and civil discussions in controversial presentations, teachers can follow the following guidelines.

Establish ground rules.

Set ground rules for discussions during presentations before conflicts arise. Many teachers do this cooperatively with students. Students "buy in" to rules when they help to develop them. Students can discuss how they would, and would not, like peers to respond to contrary opinions and ideas. Do they want to allow inflammatory language, name-calling, personal attacks, and sarcasm? Most likely not, so they can agree to avoid such behavior. Students should also know what discussions are for — understanding and thoughtful analysis. Introducing discussion techniques like turn-taking ensures that every student will have the opportunity to participate.

Promote active listening.

Teaching paraphrasing and perception checking are excellent devices for setting up civil discussions. Some teachers require students to restate the teacher's opinion during presentations and other students' opinion during follow-up discussions. Paraphrases need to be accurate before a student may state an opposing opinion. This encourages students to communicate opinions clearly.

Focus on perspective and diversity.

Instead of students expressing how they feel about an issue, they can discuss why different types of people might feel differently about the issue. Every issue has multiple perspectives, and the strategy requires students to consider them. Many textbooks encourage multiple perspectives, including interviews with people from diverse backgrounds. Teachers often find it useful to pair students in dyads for discussion. Students may not conflict but they will still offer different perspectives on a given issue. Dyads are great testing grounds for practicing ground rules and making situations more interpersonal.

Recognize emotions.

Students want to share personal stories and feelings. Teachers should be prepared for students to be emotional and try to make space for it. On the other hand, the point of learning is to understand the experiences of people who are not like us. Students are encouraged to support opinions with evidence, rather than simply relying on strong emotions and personal experience. Students benefit from setting feelings aside and moving beyond them. Learning can then take place.

Use readings to guide discussions.

Using readings about controversial issues allows students to see how others think about the issues. Statements and even single quoted sentences help to get thinking and discussions started when students are hesitant to voice an opinion.

Avoid dualistic thinking.

Every issue has two sides, often more than two. William Perry (1981) developed a model of thinking based upon the work of Jean Piaget that outlines how student thinking can move from "right or wrong" to an appreciation of multiplicity. Teachers can model multiplicity thinking during presentations and encourage it by addressing "fallacies of thinking."

Deal with conflict.

Despite a teacher's best efforts, student emotions can get out of hand. There are strategies useful for managing active conflict. Teachers can call a "time out" to give students a chance to calm down. Teacher comments like "We've stopped listening to one another" help create a different perspective and remind students of ground rules. Rephrasing student comments in less emotional terms helps focus students on content and analysis. Finally, asking students to reflect on what is happening in the discussion and on the nature of the disagreement is also useful.

PLANNING THE ORAL PRESENTATION

This section offers teachers insight into the process of planning an effective oral presentation. It focuses on the importance of the teacher's relationship with the student audience and suggests strategies for making an impact. An effective presentation makes the best use of the relationship between the teacher and the students, and it takes student needs into consideration. It helps teachers to capture interest, develop understanding, and achieve learning objectives.

Topic Selection

A well-selected presentation topic can mean the difference between student engagement and apathy. As stressed earlier, a teacher needs to be well acquainted with the nature of the student audience. Teachers need to select a topic that students can relate to and that will secure their attention. By delving a little deeper into students' circumstances, teachers are able to modify topics for maximum effect. For example, research may reveal that a class is made up of students who want to be elementary school teachers. Focusing too much on secondary or college teaching would be impractical.

Have knowledge and passion.

By selecting a topic about which a teacher holds a degree of knowledge, there is less research time and more available time to concentrate on making the presentation stimulating. Topics on which teachers are already well acquainted can be presented with more confidence and credibility by including personal experiences. Of course, teachers should also present on subjects for which they have passion. Passion and enthusiasm are contagious. If teachers speak on a subject that excites them, their fervor helps to keep students alert and engaged. And teachers model learning.

In addition, subtopics that are relevant to the teacher and students can give a subject far more personal appeal. For example, when delivering a talk on the future of educational technology, part of the topic can be dedicated to smartphones, to which many students (and teachers) have a hopeless addiction. By so doing, a teacher blends facts and statistics with a healthy dose of relatedness.

Consider the purpose.

Teachers should reflect carefully on the purpose of an oral presentation before settling on a topic and title. What should students learn? What is the learning objective? Is the objective of the presentation practical, offering something future educators can use in the classroom? Or is the objective theoretical, offering information about an issue that affects teachers at the national level? The objective drastically affects the tone and air of the entire presentation. Either way, teachers should base the topic on a limited goal. They cannot cover an entire topic in one presentation. By crafting the topic in accordance with limitations, teachers give students the chance to grasp ideas far more effectively than they would do otherwise.

Reflecting "letting learning happen," teachers are advised to avoid either being too strongly in favor of a concept or against it, and they should give pros and cons to consider. If teachers offer different perspectives throughout the presentation and end with thoughtful questions, students are left with choices. But letting learning happen does not mean hiding one's perspective. Whichever side of the fence teachers land on, there should be data supporting different positions and evidence for opposing views with statistics and examples.

The Learning Objective

A learning objective describes what students should know or be able to do at the end of the presentation. Learning objectives should be about student behavior. Good learning objectives are not too abstract (e.g., *"Students should be able to list . . ."* is more concrete than *"Students should understand that . . ."*). I will look at higher thinking skills when I discuss Bloom's taxonomy in the next chapter. The learning objective supports the overarching goal of the presentation and is the thread that unites all the elements or main points of the presentation.

Write clear learning objectives.

Teachers can find plenty of models for writing learning objectives. The point is to keep it simple and focus on objectives that speak to the knowledge and skills students need to learn. First, what should students be able to do by the end of the presentation? Second, what should students know and understand by the end of the presentation? To help identify the skills and knowledge students should gain throughout the presentation, sentences should begin with the phrase "After this presentation, students will be able to . . ." and end with phrases like the examples here:

- . . . list the elements of Steiner's approach to positive discipline.
- . . . identify the advantages and disadvantages of the voucher system.
- . . . explain the difference between cooperative and collaborative learning.
- . . . have observable outcomes.

Each example above uses an active verb that defines desired student behavior in a specific way. A teacher can observe whether a student can list, identify, or explain something. As teachers create learning objectives, they need to think about what observable evidence students can provide to demonstrate mastery of the objective. Phrases like "understand," "become familiar with," "show appreciation for," and "develop the necessary skills for" are ambiguous. It's the difference between a learning objective that states, "Students will know the major theories of conflict resolution" and one that reads, "Students will list the five major approaches to theories of conflict resolution."

Research Strategy

Researching a presentation is a very different process than researching a paper. People read a report and can go back and forth in the written text. They cannot do that with an oral presentation. A presentation should show a teacher's mastery of the topic and demonstrate how the teacher has organized, clarified, and advanced a body of knowledge.

Following are some tips for making presentation research more effective and efficient.

Plan ahead

For a presentation, teachers are required to do thorough, scholarly research—this cannot be done in a day or a weekend. Teachers should allow enough time to find, read, and analyze research materials before outlining the final presentation. They need time to get to know the issue and information. They have to live with it for a while.

Keep track of research.

There are many ways to keep track of research either electronically on a laptop or in a paper notebook. However, teachers need to keep a *research log*. They need to track where they've been as they did the research. Teachers should provide complete citations of all materials used in the presentation and use the research log to make notes about the location of useful materials and how they will be used in the presentation. The research log is also a good place to archive sources in order to go back later and refine with additional research and analysis.

Stay focused on the topic.

One of the easiest mistakes to make is to find and read interesting materials that are not directly relevant to the topic and get sidetracked. If teachers think the information may be useful later, they can make a note in the research log. Teachers should stay focused on what they need to research at the stage they are in. They can always go back to other information later.

Keep electronic research credible.

Doing an electronic search is becoming the most common way for teachers to research presentations. The search process is keyword driven, and results depend on the relevance of words entered into a search engine like Google, Yahoo, or Bing. Search engines identify all records containing the word or words entered into the search fields. Depending on the word combination, keywords lead to various books, articles, and Web pages with various degrees of usefulness. Consequently, it's very important to learn how to shape a search. Teachers need to try a number of descriptors—subject headings and subheadings—about a topic to find the most productive path.

It is crucial to assess the credibility of electronic sources based on the connection of the author to the subject, the intended audience, sources of information, and supporting evidence. Many search engines rank material according to what is relevant, but that doesn't mean the material is reliable. Teachers should check sources for bias and choose sources that show some sensitivity to both sides of an issue.

It is important to remember that failure to cite electronic sources on presentation outlines and visual slides, or orally during the presentation, whether deliberately or inadvertently, is an act of *plagiarism*. Ignorance of academic regulations or the excuse of running out of time does not constitute an acceptable defense against the charge of plagiarism. The Internet is full of sites where teachers get information on how to correctly cite electronic sources through either the APA or MLA approach.

Five-Paragraph Outline

A teacher cannot create a strong oral presentation without an outline. The so-called five paragraph outline is a blueprint that makes planning and delivering the presentation much easier. Teachers develop an outline after they do research on a subject. Otherwise, they cannot preview the information that must be included in the presentation. In addition, the five-paragraph outline is a substitute for note cards, which can be problematic. I don't know how many times I have seen speakers drop note cards and interrupt their presentation. A five-paragraph (or five-section) approach keeps the presentation on track and encourages teachers to know the topic.

The more detailed the outline is, the easier it will be for teachers to expand it into a complete presentation. A five-paragraph outline guides a presentation. It requires three main points that fit the learning objective. Adding subpoints is necessary. The outline includes the following:

1. Introduction

    - A "hook" to captures the students' attention
    - The topic of the presentation
    - The learning objective
    - The three main points of the presentation that help students to follow the organization of the presentation

2. Main point #1

    - Main point #1 and background information on the topic

3. Main point #2:

    - Main point #2 usually offers one side of the issue and the evidence to support it
    - Sub point contains statistics, stories or examples to support main point #2
    - Another sub point if necessary

4. Main point #3

- Main point #3 and offers the other side of the issue and the evidence to support it
- Sub point contains statistics, stories or examples to support main point #3
- Another sub point if necessary

5. Conclusion

- Restate the learning objective
- Review the three main points of the presentation
- Conclude with a summary or quotation that encourages audience to think about the issue

Use a keyword outline.

There are two common formats of outlines: *full sentence* and *keyword*. The first type implies that outlines should consist of complete sentences. Although more thorough, it does not encourage teachers to know the subject and speak from their own knowledge. However, at an early stage of presentation development, a full-sentence approach can make the presentation much easier. Teachers only need to add some evidence to every argument in order to complete it.

The second format uses keywords when developing various points of the outline. This approach is most beneficial for urging speakers to know the subject matter. Speaking from a keyword outline during the oral presentation keeps a teacher on track and pressures him or her to talk about the topic, not read from notes. The teacher expands keywords into sentences and phrases. One concern teachers have about keyword outlines is the lack of room on a one-page outline for detailed information. This concern can be alleviated by using visual slides as additional sources of information. Not all information has to be on the outline. Some can be communicated through visual aids. Teachers can balance information between the outline and visual slides.

The ideal approach is to make a full-sentence outline and then translate it into a keyword outline for the actual presentation. In the vast majority of cases, there are no specific formatting requirements for a five-paragraph outline. This means that teachers can write the outline however they like. But a major theme of this book is about the conversational nature of teacher communication. A keyword outline promotes a conversational tone to teacher presentations and helps teachers to be more relational. An outline should be flexible to allow a teacher to converse about a topic and not just read lines. If teachers have taken the time to thoroughly research a topic and have lived with the topic, they can talk about the topic. They know the topic well enough to converse. A key-

word outline prepares teachers to give presentations whereby they produce unique knowledge and not just reproduce information.

DELIVERING THE ORAL PRESENTATION

After analyzing the rhetorical situation and planning the presentation,
it's time to deliver it. Delivery is what most teachers have in mind when
thinking about presentations. The most important thing to remember
about delivery is that it should help students to understand what is being
said. Effective presentations are about communication, not performance.
Thinking of presentations as dialogue rather than soliloquy helps teachers achieve a keen sense of communication. All aspects of delivery should
promote conversational quality and focus on communicating meaning.
Teachers use the following techniques as means to student learning.

Capture Attention

The first step of delivering an effective oral presentation is to capture
student attention and increase engagement. This is called "the hook."
Robert J. Marzano (2015) suggests a number of ways for engaging students in presentations. They include the following:

Encourage physical movement.

Marzano observes that the same part of the brain that processes movement also processes learning. During presentations, teachers should find
ways to incorporate movement—both for themselves and for the student
audience. Starting with a story is itself an effective hook but is even more
so when the teacher moves naturally from side to side and back and forth
in the classroom. It doesn't have to be dramatic. It just requires that
students follow "the action." Asking students to respond to an initial
question by getting up out of their seats and standing with students of
the same opinion also utilizes physical movement to engage attention.

Entice with missing information.

Curiosity and anticipation grab students' attention. Showing what
students don't know but what they may need to know can be an effective
hook. For example, showing a brief one-to-two-minute video of a teacher
using a disciplinary technique effectively reminds students who want to
be teachers of what they will be facing every day.

Raise mild controversy.

Students enjoy controversy if not too strong. It captures attention by
adding excitement and fun to the classroom. In a master's program

course, an education professor began the class with the Pink Floyd song *The Wall* and the lyrics, "Hey! Teachers! Leave them kids alone!" It raised the issue of teacher authority (and its abuse) and captured student attention.

Ask questions.

Students raise their level of attention if requested to respond to a question. Mild pressure can be good for generating responses. Try to get several points of view to sharpen students' thinking. Don't forget to provide adequate *wait time* before calling on the next student. Allow at least three seconds before calling for the next response. Build anticipation and tension with the three-second-pause rule for students to respond.

Preview and Review

One technique applied in an oral presentation to enhance learning is for the teacher to preview and review the main points. The preview happens in the introduction to the presentation. The purpose of the preview is to let students get an idea of what is to come before the actual event occurs. Cognitive psychologists call the preview an *advanced organizer*. If teachers preview the main points, students are more likely to remember the material after the presentation. In other words, they are more likely to store it in memory by attaching it to items previously learned.

The other half of the technique is the review, which happens at the start of the conclusion and refreshes the minds of students about the main points covered during the body of the presentation. It reviews the main points and reflects the old speech adage, "Tell them what you are going to say, then tell them, and then tell them what you said." Oral presentations, unlike written essays, require redundancy to help listeners follow the presentation and understand. A reader of a written text has the luxury of going back and rechecking ideas; a student listening to an oral presentation does not.

Use Visual Aids

Visual aids are another tool to help students follow the presentation and understand information. Visual aids allow students time to understand and process what is being said. Visual aids do not immediately disappear into thin air to be forgotten, as spoken words or hand gestures do. They can be sequenced to break down and present ideas bit by bit. They allow for clarifying images and consistent memories.

One type of visual aid is a physical object or thing. Objects and things are excellent visuals to use for speakers with anxiety and apprehension about presenting. They can help decenter a speaker, taking some focus off the speaker and putting it on the object. For example, teachers can give a brief presentation at the beginning of a course to introduce themselves by bringing a personal object from home that they believe represents them in some way. The object can be anything, such as a gold pocket watch given to a teacher by a grandparent. The watch can represent quality, time, and family; and the teacher can explain how he or she relates to the values of always doing one's best, using time wisely, and appreciating connections to family. The important thing is that the object is a matter of concern to the teacher, something of emotional value with a sense of personal association. Often objects have such emotional power that the presentation becomes larger than the speaker, who gets caught up in the emotional connection and forgets that he or she is presenting.

Be Conversational

Dialogue, or conversation, is among two or more people. A conversational style promotes a sense of connectedness and a community of practice in an oral presentation and helps to develop effective learning relationships. It entails a particular kind of teacher–student interaction. As Nicholas Burbules (1993) argues, it is "at heart a kind of social relation that engages its participants." It entails certain virtues and emotions, like some of Barbules's examples that follow.

Concern and affection

Conversation is a sense of being with others in communication and engages students in thought and discussion. There is more going on in conversation than lecturing about an overt topic. There is a social bond that entails concern, interest and commitment to the student audience. Conversational presentations involve feelings for students. Nel Noddings (1992) points out that teachers express concern by verbal and nonverbal behavior, occasionally asking students if they understand or have questions. They show approachability, humility and friendliness.

Trust and risk

Students often have to take what teachers are saying on faith—there is some risk in this. Trust is essential to student well-being and educational success, but it cannot occur without accepting the possibility of betrayal. The need for trust arises from the interdependence with others in learning. Students depend on other students and teachers to help them obtain the outcomes educators promote and value. As student interests intertwine, there is an element of risk insofar as students encounter learning situations where they must trust in order to learn. Trust is crucial in instructional interactions and educational communities of practice.

Respect and appreciation

While there may be large differences between teachers and student partners, the process of giving an oral presentation is only conversational if there is mutual regard and respect. This involves establishing a prevailing idea that everyone is equal in some basic way and entails teacher commitment to being fair-minded—opposing degrading students and rejecting the use of sarcasm and humiliation.

Respect also includes appreciation of the unique qualities that students bring to the presentation. Having a diverse group of students requires recognizing that all students are unique in their own way. Their differences consist of academic level, cultural background, personality, religious beliefs, and so forth. There is always diversity in the classroom and in today's society, it is important to embrace it and make positive use of it. Teachers should value diversity and model this attitude to their students during the oral presentation. When teachers value uniqueness and diversity, they recognize different perspectives and respect the fact that students have different opinions. Differences are generally a good thing in thinking through issues.

CONCLUSION

This chapter argued that oral presentations should promote effective learning relationships and communities of practice, and help students learn about a subject matter, about themselves, and about relating to others. Learning about content, self-identity, and others is actively promoted by effective oral presentations through student participation and conversation. Mutual communication is a fundamental part of oral presentations. A balanced relationship of communicative interaction benefits teachers and students alike. Through student participation and dialogue, teachers plan and deliver oral presentations that help create a community of practice; learning becomes a valued collective endeavor and promotes effective learning relationships.

ELEVEN

Instructional Discussions

"Instructional discussion is a classroom teaching method by which students move through material to a predetermined, new understanding by building on each other's contributions." —*Jody Nyquist*

One of the challenges for new teachers is developing the ability to guide students through class discussions. Discussion is a highly effective teaching method that encourages students to share opinions and ask questions. It provides a means for students to clarify information in readings, videos, and lectures. Students can share ways for explaining information, concepts, and principles. Most important, teachers use discussion to emphasize active rather than passive learning.

One particularly active method is *instructional discussion*, as introduced by Jody Nyquist (1975). Instructional discussion is a classroom teaching strategy whereby students listen to a brief lecture and reach the learning objective by discussing a set of prepared questions. This chapter describes the characteristics of instructional discussions, outlines questions based on Benjamin Bloom's taxonomy that generate student thinking (knowledge, comprehension, application, analysis/synthesis, and evaluation), and provides a plan for teachers who want to try the method.

PLANNING THE INSTRUCTIONAL DISCUSSION

The idea of instructional discussions is not new. Educators have long talked about engaging students in interactions to promote analysis, reflection, and critical thinking. The great teachers of ancient Greece used what Edward Gordon (1990) calls a "conversational form" of teaching. Discussion might appear simply as interaction between teachers and students, but it offers a rich instructional method. Instructional discussions engage students. They make ideas relevant. They provide themes that run throughout the discussion and encourage high levels of student participation.

Instructional discussion is a teaching method that blends lectures and discussions. The instructor predetermines a learning objective that students reach through responding to a set of questions. The steps necessary for effectively planning the instructional discussion method are (1) *organize* the instructional discussion, including an outline and a clear and concrete learning objective; (2) *identify* background information; (3) *create questions* that help student thinking to reach the learning objective; (4) *anticipate*themes of the discussion; and (5) *prepare* interavtive visual aids.

Organize the Instructional Discussion

Instructional discussions are more challenging than they first appear. Many teachers assume that discussions should happen naturally. But instructional discussions demand teaching behaviors that come neither easily nor naturally. Teachers need to develop a clear and concise learning objective and select themes to focus student discussion. They also need to provide background information that will help students discuss the material. Background information must be understandable and accessible. Instructional discussions are a complex but rich teaching strategy.

Prepare an instructional discussion outline.

The outline of a twenty-to-fifty-minute instructional discussion begins with an introduction that includes a topic statement and a review of relevant background. The review is different than the preview suggested in chapter 10. The review highlights information necessary for students to fully respond to discussion questions. The information comes from a previous lecture or from new material.

Instructional discussions develop higher-order thinking that requires students to apply ideas to real-life situations, analyze problems, synthesize solutions, and evaluate the usefulness of information. Bloom's (1956) taxonomy is applied to a learning objective through its six levels of thinking that begin with basic knowledge of a subject and move toward more complex critical analysis. The levels include the following:

1. *Knowledge*—the basic recall of facts, such as a student restating the dictionary definition of a word.
2. *Comprehension*—a student articulating the meaning of a word, concept, or principle in their own words.
3. *Application* —applying a concept to a new situation.
4. *Analysis*—breaking a problem or issue into component parts and looking for patterns or generalizations.

5. *Synthesis* — putting those components back together in new ways.
6. *Evaluation* — arguing the worth or value of information or knowledge.

With Bloom's six levels of critical thinking, teachers develop learning objectives for higher-order thinking like application, analysis/synthesis, and evaluation. Although knowledge and comprehension levels are typically addressed in a previous lecture, the instructional discussion moves students beyond basic thinking skills to application, synthesis, and evaluation.

Create a learning objective.

Creating a clear and concrete learning objective depends on teacher expectation of what students will know or be able to do at the end of the instructional discussion. Learning objectives are written in terms of learning outcomes: What should students learn or be able to do as a result of the discussion? A three-step process leads teachers to clear and concrete learning objectives.

First, teachers create a learning objective *stem*. Objectives typically start with a phrase such as "Upon completion of this course, students will/should be able to . . ." Other examples of stems include "After completing the discussion, the student will be able to . . ."or "After this discussion, the student will have . . ." Worthy stems also include: "By completing the discussion, the student will . . ." and "At the conclusion of the discussion, the student will . . ."

Second, teachers add an *active verb*, such as *analyze, recognize, compare, provide*, or *list* to the stem. Action verbs can be observed. They should reflect Bloom's six levels of thinking. Here are some examples:

- Knowledge
  - *Define . . .*
  - *List . . .*
- Comprehension
  - *Illustrate . . .*
  - *Describe . . .*
- Application
  - *Apply . . .*
  - *Use . . .*
- Analysis
  - *Compare . . .*
  - *Contrast . . .*

- Synthesis

  - *Summarize . . .*
  - *Integrate . . .*

- Evaluation

  - *Critique . . .*
  - *Assess . . .*

Third, teachers determine the product, process, or outcome of the learning objective, such as "After completing the discussion, the student will be able to apply examples of culturally responsive teaching to classroom teaching."

Other examples of outcomes include the following:

- Discuss the differences and similarities between educational philosophies.
- Explain the strengths and weaknesses of American schooling.
- Describe three major features of progressive education philosophy.
- List four education philosophers and explain their application to teaching.
- Draw parallels between bullying and aspects of American culture.

Identify relevant background information.

The next step of the introduction identifies important points from previous lectures or new information that students need to fully respond to instructional discussion questions. It's a reminder about ideas that students will build on and apply to real-life situations. Before a discussion begins, students need to remember factual information (the knowledge and comprehension levels of Bloom's taxonomy) that will be the basis of responses to high-level questions. For example, if the learning objective is to explain the differences and similarities between education philosophies, the background information would include definitions of various education philosophies.

The introductory part of the outline looks like this:

1. Introduction

   - Topic: *John Holt's philosophy of education*
   - Learning Objective: *After the discussion, students will be able to analyze the pros and cons of John Holt's philosophy of education for the American school system*
   - Review of Background Information:

     a. *Who was John Holt?*
     b. *What is Holt's concept of "unschooling?"*
     c. *What is the dark side of John Holt?*

Develop questions to push student thinking.

Bloom's taxonomy helps teachers to use a high-order questioning strategy with application, analysis, synthesis, and evaluation questions. Application questions ask students to apply information to various situations. Analysis and synthesis questions ask students to take a problem apart and put it back together in a new way. Evaluation questions ask students to explain the value of the information in their own words.

High-order questions avoid yes-or-no responses but should not be so open-ended that they lead discussions down less relevant areas. Teachers should avoid ambiguous or vague questions such as "What did you think of John Holt's philosophy?" Questions should be clear, specific, and use vocabulary that students understand. They should help students understand concepts and help teachers judge the level of student understanding.

The body of the outline includes questions, like this:

1. Question #1 (Application Level)

    a. *What concerns of John Holt's educational philosophy to classroom experiences have you observed?*

2. Question #2 (Analysis Level)

    a. A. *What are the elements of Holt's concept of "unschooling?"*

3. Question #3 (Evaluation Level)

    a. A. *What changes to Holt's philosophy would you recommend and why?*

Anticipate themes of the discussion.

Instructional discussions are a form of theme-based teaching. They help students generate themes about a topic and engage in active learning. Instructional discussions use students' prior experience, bring relevance to student learning, facilitate deeper understanding of content, and act as springboards for student application and analysis.

The teacher should anticipate themes that may result from the questions of the discussion. For example, building on the topic of John Holt's educational philosophy, an instructional discussion could focus on the theme of student-centered approaches to teaching. Through questioning, students could generate further themes like learner autonomy, lifelong learning, problem-solving, active learning, and the construction of meaning that the teacher will highlight in the conclusion.

Prepare interactive visual aids.

Sometimes it's true that a picture is worth a thousand words. Visual aids are a useful part of an effective instructional discussion. They help learners retrieve and remember information and are effective tools for teacher communication. In particular, interactive visuals enhance student perceptions of the teacher's credibility and increase teacher confidence. Ian Parker (2001) observes that interactive visual aids can be an impressive antidote to fear—converting public-speaking dread into "moviemaking pleasure."

Effective instructional discussions require that teachers record student comments in order to identify themes. In the past, teachers used the board, flip charts, or overhead projectors to list ideas. Today's teachers have access to interactive visual tools like PowerPoint and Smart Boards. Interactive white boards allow teachers to boost student engagement, motivation, and retention by using digital resources and student ideas. They help teachers engage students by reflecting their ideas back at them and archiving a class discussion.

Unlike a traditional white board, interactive tools catalog individual student responses and how they contribute to major themes. Discussions are more collaborative. Teachers create visual slides with questions at the top and write down student responses on the slide during the discussion. Teachers list student feedback and make notes. Student responses are saved so that a teacher can go back and review comments for themes. Through interactive visual aids, discussions illustrate the co-construction of meaning by teachers and students.

Finally, teachers should follow a few tips about using interactive visual aids in instructional discussions:

- Standardize slide colors, styles, and fonts.
- Use key words and leave room for student responses.
- Make content of slides self-evident.
- Use colors that contrast but that don't hide words.
- Be consistent with effects, transitions, and animation.
- Don't use too many slides, you can lose your audience's attention.
- Talk to students, not to slides.

FACILITATING THE INSTRUCTION DISCUSSION

Instructional discussions are dynamic. Teachers emphasize key points, paraphrase, check student perceptions, give students time to think, manage time, and select themes. Teachers identify students' themes to make broader sense of the discussion. Teachers make student contributions understandable to all by the following communication behaviors:

Emphasizing key points.

Teachers can use the following techniques to help students identify key ideas.

- Be explicit—For example, announce, "Susan made an important point." Teachers often do this by saying, "This will be on the exam."
- Pause—Take a few seconds just before and after making a key point. A pause has an effect and can illustrate thinking. It gives time for student to respond.
- Move—Go to a different place in the classroom. Then stop and deliver the important idea.
- Make eye contact—Don't read from a slide. That should be done before making the point. Look students in the eye and say it with meaning.
- Smile—Students respond to the immediacy of friendliness and approachability.

Paraphrasing students' comments

Paraphrasing ensures that the teacher gets the correct sense of student messages. A good paraphrase is concise and uses key words. When teachers write student responses on the board, they are often too wordy. If there are too many words, messages get lost. In instructional discussions, teachers want to accurately reflect student comments. A good paraphrase summarizes the student's response, cuts through the clutter, and focuses on the essence of the student's ideas. This helps teachers to develop a sense of what is central to a student's message.

Checking student perceptions.

Perception checking is similar to paraphrasing but more strongly focused on student feelings. It checks out the emotions that motivate a student's responses. The concern isn't as much with what the student communicated (content) as much as it is with how the student conveys the content (tone). For example, if a student is consistently quiet during a discussion, a teacher might assume that the student doesn't care much about the topic. If the teacher checks out this perception, he or she might find that the student cares greatly about the topic but is insecure in discussions. Understanding the student's feeling of frustration can lead a teacher to see the real problem is associated with a safe discussion environment.

Give students time to think.

The concept of "wait-time" as an instructional strategy was invented by Mary Budd Rowe (1987). She found that the periods of silence between teacher questions and students' responses rarely lasted more than one and a half seconds in typical classrooms. She discovered that when teachers don't answer their own questions but wait at least three seconds, positive things happen to students' behaviors and attitudes. The length of student responses increases. The number of student "I don't know" and no answer responses decreases. And the number of volunteered, appropriate answers by larger numbers of students greatly increases.

Manage time.

It is important to suggest appropriate time schedules for instructional discussions. Teachers need to limit discussions to certain time frames. Teachers watch the clock and remind students about the time remaining. A typical instructional discussion consists of five minutes of introduction that includes sharing the topic, the objective, and a review of important information. If the time allotted for discussion is twenty to thirty minutes, the amount of time for responses to each question should be five to seven minutes. A fifty-minute class can have ten minutes of introduction, ten minutes of responses to each question, and ten minutes of conclusion with a summary of themes.

Conclude with student themes.

When teachers use "connecting to a discussion theme" strategies like instructional discussions, they establish connections between student comments and larger themes. Consider discussing curiosity in John Holt's *How Children Fail*. Holt (1995) argues that fear, humiliation, punishment, and failure destroy natural curiosity and learning in children. A "connecting to a discussion theme" strategy could include themes like teacher–student relationships, positive discipline, realistic expectations, respect, and alternative education. By using instructional discussions, teachers show the development of individual perspectives into a community of practice.

CONCLUSION

This chapter presented instructional discussion as a highly effective teaching method that encourages students to express opinions and develop high-order thinking. It provides a means by which students clarify information from readings, videos, lectures, and other learning materials. It allows students to generate their own responses to questions. Most important, the teaching method emphasizes a commitment to active rather than passive learning and to mutual communication as a fundamental part of a classroom. Through student participation and exchanges, instructional discussions help learning become a valued collective endeavor.

TWELVE

Online Communication

It's not the tech; it's how the tech is used. —*Preston Smith*

A teacher is preparing to instruct students in an online college, high school, or even a middle school class. Like other social situations—families, educational institutions, corporations, industrial businesses, social service agencies, governmental departments, church meetings, and special interest groups—online classrooms have potential for developing communities of practice and effective learning relationships. In the online environment, teaching means taking command of the technical aspects of communication and relating to online students as people.

This chapter introduces teachers to the particular needs of online teaching and learning. It is not technically oriented, with the latest technological "bells and whistles." As Preston Smith (2014), president of Rocketship Education, observes, "I'm here to tell you technology, on its own, is no cure." Online education may purposefully integrate learning and technology in a manner that creates an educational experience, but it alone is no guarantee of success. Online teaching only succeeds when implemented by teachers who understand the particular communication needs of the technological learning environment. This chapter focuses on the relational elements of online education. It sees the online classrooms as having potential for effective learning relationships and communities of practice.

BENEFITS OF ONLINE EDUCATION

The Association for Supervision and Curriculum Development (2015), which has the goal of developing and delivering innovative programs, products, and services that empower educators to support the success of

137

learners, outlines some of the benefits of online education. First, online teaching and learning saves money and resources. Although online classes can be more time-consuming and labor-intensive than traditional classes, they eliminate the need for teachers and students to travel to school, reducing transportation costs, and are less expensive than on-site education.

Second, online courses give teachers and students access to online teaching and learning opportunities anytime and anyplace from the comfort of home and to a beach on a summer or holiday break. Third, online education increases student accountability. It is more accountable than traditional education because assignments, assessment scores, activities, course completions, and student progress can be archived online.

Fourth, online teaching can be interpersonal (White and Weight, 2000) and bring education to life. When online teachers take full advantage of the interactivity and multimedia power of the electronic classroom, they engage students with virtual classroom scenes, interviews, and demonstrations. The variety of methods and activities offers valuable learning experiences not always practiced in solely textbook-based courses. Online education can create excitement about learning. Interactivity and multimedia can make learning engaging and fun for students.

But no matter the benefits (and limitations), online education is the wave of the present and it behooves teachers to gain the necessary communication attitudes and skills to succeed in the environment.

TAKING COMMAND OF ONLINE COMMUNICATION

As chapter 1 stressed, communication is inherently complex. Seeking a single definition of online communication is not as productive as identifying its major components. One way to address the issue is to go back to the two general functions of communication as described by Conrad and Poole (2012). The command and the relational functions relate to online communication.

To review, a *command* is any message that influences students to take action or to accept certain ideas. In online classrooms, command communication helps teachers to direct the inherently complex learning environment that is full of possible misunderstandings. At a minimum, online communication requires command communication in order for teachers to issue clear and effective instructions. Online instructors issue commands by clearly describing actions and prescribing the limits of actions. Clear and precise commands are necessary for online students to understand and limit actions to specific steps.

Online command communication is both descriptive and prescriptive. Clear instructions must be descriptive before being transmitted as an online message. The online student must easily decode the message and transform it into specific behavior. The transmission and reception of the message should correspond as closely as possible to both meaning and prescribed behavior and tell the online student not only what to do but how to do it. For example, an online teacher may want more interaction in class discussions. The teacher describes the action of discussion but does not clearly prescribe specific student behavior. What does *discussion* mean in an online environment? Does an online student response like "I agree" count? Should online students be encouraged to post more substantive replies to other students' content-related messages? The online teacher needs to clearly prescribe action by posting a message like: "Effective online interaction goes beyond simple 'I agree' messages. It moves a discussion forward by asking for clarification, offering a personal experience, giving examples or integrating comments into a new idea."

Description and prescription are absolutely necessary for effective online instructions, as they influence the capability of online students to successfully achieve course objectives. Many online instructors start with the following simple techniques:

- Think about the wording and clarity of instructions. Ask: Would I clearly understand these instructions if given to me? Do they accurately reflect my instructional goals and objectives?
- Write short instructions and edit out complex language. Is there language that distracts from the goals and objectives?
- Give logical instructions by using prescriptive language. Is the language prescriptive as well as descriptive. Does it help online students through the steps to successfully accomplish the objective? Does it offer a model of what the online students should be doing?

Even the meaning of simple online commands and instructions can be hampered because online communication process is inherently verbal. Although online students receive a clearly written transmission of an online message, the lack of face-to-face contact and nonverbal communication influence the achievement of meaning. Online students hold a diversity of perceptions, values, prejudices, biases, attitudes, levels of education, and opinions. Different understandings naturally occur online because of the diversity of students. Consequently, online communication requires student feedback on the clarity and understanding of instructions.

Like other educators, online teachers often assume that students understand if instructions are transmitted clearly. This assumption is especially strong when teachers issue a set of routine instructions. Comfortable in the knowledge that commands are transparent, teachers expect students to take the actions and accomplish the learning task. But without numerous forms of student feedback, online teachers experience misunderstandings. Online teaching adjustments cannot be made unless there is feedback from students about whether instructions are understood. By regularly checking for student understanding, online teachers can clarify instructions and encourage mutual understanding. Two specific techniques already mentioned can also improve the command function of online communication and facilitate online student feedback: paraphrasing and perception checking.

Online Paraphrasing

Online paraphrasing checks student understanding by asking online students to restate some portion of course content. Different interpretations of online communication are numerous particularly if instructions are long and complex. Online paraphrasing ensures that online students get the sense of a message or information sent by the teacher. Online paraphrasing should be concise. When online students begin paraphrasing, they are often too wordy. If a paraphrase is too long, understanding is not clear. Concise paraphrases summarize student understandings and cut through clutter. They focus on what is central to ideas. As a result, online teachers understand a student's frame of reference.

For example, online paraphrasing can be used to check students' understanding of the online course syllabus. Online teachers can assign sections of the syllabus to individual students and have those students paraphrase the content in their own words. Students post the paraphrase to the class. All students get a chance to read all paraphrases. Online students can compare and contrast interpretations, and discuss differences in understanding. The online teacher joins the conversation and clarifies the intent of the information in the course syllabus. In this way, not only do online teachers know that students have read the course syllabus but they can correct misunderstandings and get all students on the same page.

Online Perception Checking

Online perception checking looks for the emotions that underlie an online student's communication. Online teachers frequently miss many of the emotional dimensions of an online conversation because they cannot see student faces and tune in to nonverbal communication. Consequently, they miss the student's personal reaction to the events of the online class. If it's true that individuality is found in feelings, online teachers miss the opportunity to sense the uniqueness of online students. For example, a student is consistently not be visible online, i.e., no posts. The student may be "lurking" in class but it is easy for the online teacher to assume that the student is not involved. If the teacher intentionally checks out the perception through a private email or phone conversation, he or she might find that the online student does not understand the importance of visibility in online classes. This leads the online teacher to see the problem as temporary because the online student is new to the online learning environment.

To summarize, the command function of online communication is a process where online instructors improve online teaching by conscious and logical steps. They do the following:

- Promote clear course instructions through descriptive language— Put thoughts or ideas into words that are simple, clear, concise and understandable to online students.
- Assist online students to understand course instructions through prescriptive language—Help online students understand by adjusting instructions and delivering them in various forms.
- Encourage online student feedback—Confirm that online course instructions have been clearly understood by students paraphrasing and the online teacher perception checking.

RELATIONAL ONLINE TEACHING

The command level of communication helps online teachers understand how to improve the technical aspect of online communication. It does not capture the full richness of online communication or account for all the relational dynamics of online teaching. It is a mistake to see that as the only level of online communication. Sending online messages is never as simple as directly transferring meaning from the online teacher to the online student. Effective online communication is not simply a matter of good mechanics, but a matter of relating with online students.

Important meaning can be found in the words or symbols used in the online classroom. Online communication is largely a matter of clear grammar. But meaning is also created in the relationships between the online teacher and students. Like any human situation, online classrooms are composed of people. Like any form of human organization, the online classroom is not always a rational, planned combination of interrelated, static components. It is made up of living, thinking, and emotional human beings—not inanimate and manipulated objects. Online classrooms are networks of interdependent relationships that have the potential, but not the guarantee, to be communities of practice.

Effective online communication is important for relational reasons. Instead of being solely command-oriented, the online teaching and learning environment is a medium of relationships and community. In the relational realm, perceptions and emotions—not tasks, commands, or logical sequences—provide the guidelines within which online students make decisions about how to act. Instead of depending solely on clarity and precision, relational communication works with uncertainty. Relational communication helps students to work through new and ambiguous information in the online environment.

Unfortunately, evidence indicates that teachers have been extremely slow to even traditional teaching as relational (Herold, 2015) despite the massive influx of new technology. Stanford University education professor Larry Cuban observes, "The introduction of computers into schools was supposed to improve academic achievement and alter how teachers taught. Neither has occurred." For the most part, teacher-centered instruction continues to be the norm in both on-site and online education.

Online education requires that teachers relate with, rather than control, the attitudes and behaviors of online students. It is a relational medium within which teachers can transform understanding and effectively coordinate interactions between themselves and online students. Like all human action, online communication is contextualized by human relationships. Good online teaching requires a relational level. Its heart and soul are ultimately found in the qualities of human relationships. If personal relationships and communication are not effective, online communication is denied the establishment of communities of practice and effective learning relationships.

One Cannot NOT Communicate Online

Online command communication is intentional, purposeful, and rationally motivated. But online relational communication happens even when online instructors and students don't think they are communicating. It's easy to see this in face-to-face situations. Teachers see students nodding heads during a lecture. Although students don't know that they are communicating with the teacher, they are communicating a great deal—interest, engagement, and a desire to understand. These students are communicating whether they think so or not.

Online communication is also inevitable. Like Joseph DeVito (2008) declares about all communication, online teachers and students *cannot NOT communicate*. The online environment includes forms of nonverbal communication. Presence, visibility, and timing make online communication inevitable and always happening. The issue for online teachers is how to exert some positive effect on online forms of nonverbal communication. Although online teachers can make written commands clearer and more precise in order to encourage student understanding, they cannot control all aspects of online communication. But they can use them to their advantage. Teachers have been reluctant to see teaching as relational despite the influx of student-centered technology, ne such online nonverbal equivalent is *tone*. The tone of online communication illustrates the increased complexity of online teaching and learning, and highlights the possibilities for teacher and student effective learning relationships.

Positive Online Tone

A significant portion of communication meaning is determined by how words are expressed. Much of online meaning is expressed by tone. Online tone is a highly speculative field and difficult to define and understand but there is no question about its importance. The *way* a message is sent is often more relevant than *what* is sent. Judgments derived from online tone are often more valid to students than judgments from the actual written words. When verbal and nonverbal online messages differ, like all people, online students tend to believe the nonverbal.

The importance of online tone cannot be overemphasized. Any seasoned online teacher can vouch for how a productive tone has a significant positive effect on perceptions of online students. Describing positive online tone in general terms is not difficult. The challenge lies in being specific about what online behaviors actually account for effective online tone. For example, most experienced online instructors have known for years that typing in all caps sets up a negative online tone. IT MAKES IT APPEAR THAT YOU ARE YELLING AT STUDENTS! Jack Gibb's (1961) idea of supportive communication offers characteristics of supportive communication and defensive-arousing communication and gives examples of positive online tone.

Gibb argues that all communication creates feelings of discomfort and defensiveness when its content is presented in a way that encourages people to feel that they are being judged, manipulated, or controlled inappropriately; deceived into believing that they are having an effect on decisions when they are not; experience cold, impersonal, and uncaring treatment, treated as a relatively useless person; or lectured to by "know-it-all" authority figures. He identifies six types of destructive communication and six types of contrasting supportive communication that when applied to online communication can help to create a positive online tone, create a community of practice and develop effective learning relationships.

Descriptive, not evaluative.

What is the difference between writing to an online student, "You're not visible in class!" versus the statement, "I've missed you from class the last two days"? Both statements pertain to the same online behavior. The real difference lies in how the message is communicated. It is more supportive to describe behavior to another than it is to evaluate that behavior in an absolute fashion. It is more supportive to send "I" messages than "you" messages. "I" messages are less likely to lead to defensive behavior because they describe an online student's behavior rather than judge the online student's character.

In other words, it is more productive to be descriptive about online communication than evaluative. To evaluate an online student's behavior is to assume knowing the truth about the situation and the student. To describe an online student's behavior is qualified and tentative. It assumes that the online teacher can learn the truth about the situation and about that student.

Participatory, not controlling.

Online students become defensive when a teacher attempts to control, rather than guide, a solution or activity. The traditional statement, "You'll do it because I told you so," is probably the clearest and most extreme example of this type of controlling communication, but it makes the point. A contrasting, supportive approach is to let online students participate through choice by allowing them to choose how to respond to online assignments or how to respond to assignments. Or online students can choose the level of participation. The idea is for online teachers and students to find common ground, to find "win-win" solutions to problems, and to build a community of practice.

To online students, there is a difference between a teacher posting, "You must be visible in class!" versus the invitation, "Is there something I can do to help you feel comfortable in class"? Consequently, a key skill for inviting participation, rather than controlling the situation, is empathy. Online teachers should put themselves in the online student's shoes. No one likes to be controlled and everyone appreciates an invitation to participate. For example, online teachers can give online students a break or a benefit of the doubt by not assuming that an online student's lack of visibility is an easy way out or laziness. Some students, even today, are new to the online environment and may be unsure about expressing their opinions—all conditions that online teachers have experienced one way or another in their own lives. They can approach online students in the manner they would like to be approached.

Genuine, not manipulative.

According to Gibb, one goal of supportive communication, and likewise a positive online tone, is to avoid communicating in a manipulative way. If online teachers only concentrate on the command function of communication, they run the risk of being seen as manipulative. Supportive communication is perceived as less fixated on the task and more open to human emotion. For example, supportive communication online means *humanizing* online messages by writing in a way that shows online teachers are communicating with real people and not with computers. It shows that they care about human beings. First, online teachers should always use online students' names in messages. Second, they should share aspects of personal and professional life in a course autobiography and have online students do the same. Third, they should use humor and even techniques like emoticons. Finally, they should occasionally change the mode of communication—use the phone to communicate with online students to get a sense of their voices and personalities.

Interpersonal, not impersonal.

Remember the last time you interacted with a sterile, seemingly un-caring individual? It may have been a clerk at a bank, an administrator at a school, or even a fellow teacher. The studied neutrality of people in any setting raises defenses. But it does particularly in online classrooms. In online communication, students might relate to other people as though they are computers themselves—not unique, thinking and feeling human beings. The online situation excludes the abundant nonverbal cues on which people normally depend for linguistic meaning. Online students replace this missing information with interpretations and this leads to *flaming*—blunt and impulsive language that would never be expressed face-to-face.

In the online classroom, teachers can be guilty of indifference to the needs of online students because interpersonal distance or formality is seen as professional. It is, however, quite possible to be interpersonal with online students and still maintain professionalism. Online instruc-tors can take the middle road and be interpersonal, not too personal or impersonal. Both personal and impersonal communication are inappro-priate in the online learning environment, Interpersonal communication removes indifference from online communication and reduces student defensiveness.

Equal, not superior

Think back to a teacher you enjoyed in the past. The teacher probably made students feel as though they were "on par." Arrogant teachers, on the other hand, cause students to become defensive and set up walls to communication. All online teachers have limitations and weaknesses. No one has cornered the market on brains, talent, or general ability regard-less of their position or accomplishments. Lee Sproull and Sara Kiesler (1994) observe that many successful online programs view "people as people" rather than separating participants through labels such as "ad-ministrator" and "technologists," or as in an educator's case, "teachers" and "students." Truly supportive online teachers realize this fact and communicate to avoid messages of superiority and promote messages of equality. For example, in any online course, I share with students that I am a learner. I have my Ph.D. but no one will ever convince my wife that I am an expert in communication.

Tentative, not certain

As mentioned above, online teachers should not be too sure that they know the answer to a question or problem. Even if they are sure, they need to listen to what online students have to say. It is usually much more supportive to frame a problem or raise an issue in a tentative way, rather than from the standpoint of certainty. For example, statements such as "It appears as though . . .," "Don't you think . . .," or "I believe . . .," communicate tentativeness, equality and interpersonal connection much better than statements like "You're wrong," or "I'm right."

CONCLUSION

The concept of online tone is difficult to define. It depends on online students' feeling that their teachers encourage communication on both interpersonal and content-related topics. Supportive communication is fundamental for creating a relational communication climate in online classrooms. If online teachers fail to support the worth and competence of their students, they will not establish relational communication and a community of practice in their online classrooms. The potential success for establishing effective communication in any online classroom depends on two key aspects: practicing specific techniques of command communication, and using the principles of supportive communication to establish effective learning relationships, mutual trust, dialogue, and communities of practice.

Bibliography

PREFACE

Boyer, E. L. (1990). *Scholarship reconsidered: Priorities of the professoriate*. Princeton, NJ: Carnegie Foundation for the Advancement of Teaching.

MacNeill, N., and Sicox, S. (2006). Pedagogic leadership: An alternative view of school leadership. *Perspectives, 1*.

Maroulis, S., and Gomez, L. (2008). Does "connectedness" matter? Evidence from a social network analysis within a small-school reform. *Teachers College Record, 110 , 9*, 1901–1929.

McLaughlin, C., and Byers, R. (2001). *Personal and social development for all*. London: David Fulton.

Murphy, M., and Brown, T. (2012). Learning as relational: Intersubjectivity and pedagogy in higher education. *International Journal of Lifelong Education, 31, 5*, 643–654.

PART I

Allen, M., Witt, P. L., and Wheeless, L. R. (2006). The role of teacher immediacy as a motivational factor in student learning: Using meta-analysis to test a causal model. Communication Education, 55, 21–31.

Richmond, V. P. (2002). Teacher nonverbal immediacy: Uses and outcomes. In J. L. Chesebro and J. C. McCroskey (Eds.), *Communication for teachers*. Boston: Allyn and Bacon.

Witt, P.L., Wheeless, L.R., and Allen, M. (2004). A meta-analytical review of the relationship between teacher immediacy and student learning. Communication Monographs, 72, 184–217.

CHAPTER 1

Conrad, C., and Poole, M. S. (2012). *Strategic organizational communication in a global economy*. Malden, MA: Wiley-Blackwell.

Gadamer, H. G. (1989). *Truth and method*. New York: Crossroad Publishing.

Hurt, H. T., Scott, M. D., and McCroskey, J. C. (1978). *Communication in the classroom*. Reading, MA: Addison-Wesley.

Simpson, M. (2010). Social networking nightmares. *National Education Association*. Retrieved from www.nea.org on February 16, 2015.

CHAPTER 2

Ball, P. (2014). The surprising benefits of ambiguous language. *BBC.com*. Retrieved on March 13.

Bisel, R. S., Messersmith, A. S., and Kelley, K. M. (2012). Supervisor-subordinate communication: Hierarchical mum effect meets organizational learning. *Journal of Business Communication, 49, 2,* 128–147.

Bruneau, T. (1974). Time and nonverbal communication. Journal of Popular Culture, 8 , 658–666.

Bruneau, T. (1990). Chronemics: the study of time in human interaction. In J. DeVito and M. Hecht (Eds.), The nonverbal reader (301–311). Prospect Heights, IL: Waveland Press.

Bruneau, T., and Ishii, S. (1988). Communicative silence: East and west. World Communication, 17 , 1–33.

Devito, J., and M. Heckt (Ed.) (1999). *The nonverbal reader.* Prospect Heights, IL: Waveland Press.

Ekman, P., and Friesen, W. (1967). Head and body cures in the judgment of emotions: A reformulation. Perceptual and Motor Skills, 24 , 711–724.

Hall, E. T. (1963). Proxemics: the study of man's spacial relations and boundaries. In Iago Galdston (Ed.), Man's image in medicine and anthropology (422–445). New York, NY: International Universities Press.

Heidegger, M. (1971). *On the way to language.* New York: Harper and Row.

Lunenburg, F.C. (2010). Formal communication channels: Upward, downward, horizontal, and external. *Focus on Colleges, Universities, and Schools, 4,* 1, 1–7.

Lunenburg, F. C., and Ornstein, A. C. (2008). *Educational administration: Concepts and practices.* Belmont, CA: Thomson Higher Education.

Mehrabian, A. (1972). *Nonverbal communication.* Aldine-Atherton: Chicago, Illinois.

CHAPTER 3

Darling, A. L., and Civikly, J. M. (1987). The effects of teacher humor on student perceptions of classroom communication climate. *Journal of Classroom Interaction, 22,* 24–30.

Dreyfus, H. (1992). *What computers still can't do: A critique of artificial reason.* Boston, MA: The MIT Press.

Dwyer, K. K., Bigham, S. G., Carlson, R. E., Prisbell, M., Cruz, A. M., and Fus, D. A. (2004). Communication and connectedness in the classroom: Development of the Connected Classroom Climate Inventory. *Communication Research Reports, 21,* 264–272.

Hays, E. R. (1970). Ego-threatening classroom communication: A factor analysis of student perceptions. *Speech Teacher, 19,* 43–48.

Jablin, F. M. (1979). Superior-subordinate communication: The state of the art. *Psychological Bulletin, 86,* 6, 1201–1222.

Martin, D. J., and Loomis, K. S. (2014). *Building teachers: A constructivist approach to introducing education.* Boston, MA: Cengage.

McCroskey, J. C., Fayer, J., Richmond, V., Sulliven, A., and Barraclough, R. (1996). A multi-cultural examination of the relationship between nonverbal immediacy and affective learning. *Communication Quarterly, 44,* 297–307.

Meir, E. (2009). *The Hawthorne effect in educational research.* Retrieved from www.simbio.com on March 13, 2015.

Pearce, C. (2012, September 24). *The Hawthorne effect in schools.* Retrieved from http://colbypearce.wordpress.com.

Redding, W. C. (1972). *Communication within the organization.* New York: Industrial Communication Council, and Lafeyette, IN: Purdue Research Foundation.

Satir, V. (1988). *The new people making.* Palo Alto, CA: Science and Behavior.

Stewart, J. (Ed.) (2005). *Bridges not walls.* New York: McGraw-Hill Publishing Co.

Waldeck, J.H. (2007). Answering the question: Student perceptions of personalized education and the construct's relationship to learning outcomes. *Communication Education, 56,* 409–432.

Weick, K. (1969). *The social psychology of organizing.* Reading, MA: Addison-Wesley.

CHAPTER 4

Allen, R. R., and Brown, K. L. (1976). *Developing communication competence in children.* Skokie, IL: National Textbook.

Commission on Achieving Necessary Skills (1991). *What work requires of schools: a SCANS report for America 2000.* Washington, DC: Department of Labor.

Lewin, K. (1946) Action research and minority problems. *Journal of Social Issues, 2,* 4, 34–46

Rubin, R. B., and Feezel, J. D. (1986). Elements of teacher communication competence. *Communication Education, 35,* 254–268.

Zachary, L. J. (2011). *The mentor's guide: facilitating effective learning relationships.* San Francisco CA: Jossey-Bass.

PART II

Heidegger, M. (1968). *What is called thinking?* New York: Harper and Row.

Hellweg, S. A. (1997). Formal and informal communication networks. In Peggy Yuhas Byers (Ed.), Organizational communication: Theory and behavior (39–57). Needham Heights, MA: Allyn and Bacon.

Leavitt, H. (1951). Some effects of communication patterns on group performance. *Journal of Abnormal and Social Psychology, 46,* 38–50.

Lunenberg, F. C. (2011). Network patterns and analysis: Underused sources to improve communication effectiveness. *National Forum of Educational Administration and Supervision Journal, 28,* 4, 1–7.

Moolenaar, N. K., Sleegers, P. J. C., Karsten, S., and Daly, A. J. (2012). The social fabric of elementary schools: A network typology of social interaction among teachers. *Education Studies,* iFirst Article, 1–17.

Satir, V. (1988). *The new people making.* Palo Alto, CA: Science and Behavior.

Worth, K. (2014, March 26). A crash course in building effective learning relationships with students. *Education Week Teacher.* Retrieved from http://www.edweek.org/tm/articles/2014/03/25/ctq-worth.html.

CHAPTER 5

American Association of University Woman. (1992). *How schools shortchange girls.* Washington, D.C: AAUW Educational Foundation and National Education Association.

Gadamer, H. G. (1989). *Truth and method.* New York: Crossroad Publishing.

Gallager, E. (2013). The effects of teacher-student relationships: Social and academic outcomes of low-income middle and high school students. *Online Publication of Undergraduate Studies.* Retrieved from http://steinhardt.nyu.edu/opus/issues/2013/fall/gallagher on May 30, 2015.

Rimm-Kaufman, S., and Sandilos, L. (2015). Improving student's relationships with teachers to provide essential supports for learning. *American Psychological Association.* Retrieved from http://www.apa.org/education/k12/relationships.aspx on May 30.

Sommers, C. H. (2002). *The war against boys*. New York: Simon and Schuster.
Stewart, L., Cooper, P., and Stewart, A. (2003). *Communication and gender*. Boston, MA: Allyn and Bacon.
Wenger, E. (1998). *Communities of practice: Learning, meaning and identity*. Cambridge: Cambridge University Press.

CHAPTER 6

Acosta, J., et al. (2015). Dealing with angry parents, *Education World, July 23*. Retrieved from http://www.educationworld.com/a_admin/admin/admin474.html.
Aguilar, E. (2015). Twenty tips for developing positive relationships with parents. *Edutopia, July 21*. Retrieved from http://www.edutopia.org/blog/20-tips-developing-positive-relationships-parents-elena-aguilar.
Hradecky, L. (1994). Vice-principal's guide to effective communication. *The Canadian School Executive, September/October*, 9–13.
Kraft, M. W., and Rogers, T. (2014). The underutilized potential of teacher-to-parent communication: Evidence from a field experiment. *Harvard Kennedy School, Faculty Research Working Paper Series, October*, RWP14-049.
Lawrence-Lightfoot, S. (2004). Building bridges from school to home. *Instructor, 114 (1)*, 24–28.
National Education Association. (2012). Survey finds parent-teacher relationships strong—teachers given grade of "A." *NEA Website, April 30*. Retrieved from http://www.nea.org/home/51796.htm.
Ramasubbu, S. (2015). Using technology to enable parent teacher communication. *Huffington Post, July 21*. Retrieved from http://www.huffingtonpost.com/suren-ramasubbu/using-techology-to-enabl_b_6479766.html.

CHAPTER 7

Anderson, M. A. (2002). Communicating with your principal: The heart of the matter. *Multimedia Schools, December*. Retrieved from http://www.infotoday.com/MMSchools/nov02/anderson.htm.
Brewster, C., and Railsback, J. (2003). Building trusting relationships for school improvement: Implications for principals and teachers. *Northwest Regional Educational Laboratory, September*. Retrieved from http://educationnorthwest.org/sites/default/files/trust.pdf.
Hoyle, J. R. (Ed.) (2012). Leadership styles. *Encyclopedia of Educational Leadership and Administration*. Thousand Oakes, CA: SAGE Publications.
Lewin, K., Lippit, R., and White, R. K. (1939). Patterns of aggressive behavior in experimentally created social climates. *Journal of Social Psychology, 10*, 271–301.
Peoples, J. A. (1964). The relationship of teacher communication to principal behavior. *The Journal of Experimental Education, 32*, 4.
Prato, C. C. (2015). Make the principal your partner. *PTO Today: Helping Parent Leaders Make Schools Great, July 28*. Retrieved from http://www.ptotoday.com/pto-today-articles/article/209-make-the-principal-your-partner.
Price, H. E. (2012). Principal-teacher interactions: How effective relationships shape principal and teacher attitudes. *Educational Administration Quarterly, February, 48, 1*, 39–85.
"Site based management." (1994). *Washington State PTA*.
Smith, D. W. (2013). Who is today's principal? *The Whole Child Blog, April 25*. Retrieved from http://www.wholechildeducation.org/blog/who-is-todays-principal.

"Types of leadership styles in education." (2015). Retrieved from http://www.buzzle. com/articles/types-of-leadership-styles-in-education.html.

CHAPTER 8

Girard, K. L. (1996). Preparing teachers for conflict resolution in the schools. *ERIC Digest*. Retrieved from http://www.ericdigests.org/1996-2/conflict.html.

Satir, V. (1972). *People making*. Palo Alto, CA: Science and Behavior Books.

Siller, A. L., Coletti, S. F., Parry, D., and Rogers, M. A. (1982). Coding verbal conflict tactics: Nonverbal and perceptual correlates of the "avoidance-distributive-integrative" distinction. *Human Communication, 9*, Fall, 83–95.

Sproull, L., and Kiesler, S. (1994). *Connections: New ways of working in the networked organization*. Cambridge, MA: The MIT Press.

Stewart J., Zediker, K. E., and Witteborn, S. (2007). *Together: Communicating interpersonally*. New York: Oxford University Press.

PART III

Bitzer, L. (1968). The rhetorical situation. *Philosophy and Rhetoric, 1*, (1), 1–14.

Credaro, A. (2006). *Innovation and change in education*. Retrieved from http://www.warriorlibrarian.com/LIBRARY/innovate.html.

Hart, R. P. and Burks, D. M. (1972). Rhetorical sensitivity and social interaction. *Speech Monographs, 39*, 75–91.

Lippitt, G. L. (1969). *Organization renewal: Achieving viability in a changing world*. New York: Prentice-Hall.

CHAPTER 9

Collaborative Learning: Group Work. (2015). *Cornell University Center for Teaching Excellence*. Retrieved from http://www.cte.cornell.edu/teaching-ideas/engaging-students/collaborative-learning.html on July 31.

Davis, B. G. (1993). *Tools for Teaching*. San Francisco, CA: Jossey-Bass.

Larmer, J. (2013). Is there a best way to develop the 4cs in all students? *P21 Partnership for 21st Learning , July 10*. Retrieved from http://www.p21.org/news-events/p21blog/1249-is-there-a-best-way-to-develop-the-4cs-in-all-students.

Sarkisian, E. (2010). Working in groups: A note to faculty and quick guide for students. *Derek Bok Center for Teaching and Learning, Harvard University*. Retrieved from http://isites.harvard.edu/fs/html/icb.topic58474/wigintro.html.

Speaking of Teaching. (1999). Cooperative learning: Students working in small groups. *Stanford University Newsletter, Winter, 10,* 2.

Tuckman, B. W. (1965). Developmental sequence in small groups. *Psychological Bulletin, 63,* 6, 384–399. Retrieved from http://dx.doi.org/10.1037/h0022100.

"What Are the Benefits of Group Work?" (2015). *Carnegie Mellon Eberly Center for Teaching Excellence and Educational Innovation*. Retrieved from http://www.cmu.edu/teaching/ on July 31.

"What Can I Do to Make Group Work Meaningful?" (2015). *Teaching Effectiveness Program, Teaching and Learning Center, University of Oregon*. Retrieved from http://tep.uoregon.edu/resources/new teach/groupwork.html on July 31.

CHAPTER 10

Bateman, W. L. (1990). *Open to question: The art of teaching and learning by inquiry*. San Francisco, CA: Jossey-Bass Publishers.

Boyes, K. (2015). The teacher's workshop: Workshops for teachers. *Karen Boyes Speaker*. Retrieved from http://www.karentuiboyes.com/teachers-teacher/ on August 17.

Burbules, N. (1993) *Dialogue in teaching. Theory and practice*, New York: Teachers College Press.

Klem, A. M., and Connell, J. P. (2004). Relationships matter: Linking teacher support to student engagement and achievement. *Journal of School Health, 74*, 262–273.

Marks, H. (2000). Student engagement in instructional activity: Patterns in the elementary, middle, and high school years. *American Educational Research Journal, 37*, 153–184.

Marzano, R. J. (2015). Student engagement: 5 ways to get and keep your students' attention. *Learning Sciences Marzano Center*. Retrieved from http;//www.marzanocenter.com/blog/article/5/ways-to-get-and-keep-your-students-attention/#sthash.3yXvssGc.dpuf on August 20.

Noddings, N. (1992). *The challenge to care in schools: An alternative approach to education*. New York: Teachers College Press.

Peters, M. A. (Ed.) (2002). *Heidegger, education, and modernity*. New York: Rowman and Littlefield.

CHAPTER 11

Bloom, B. S. (Ed.) (1956) *Taxonomy of Educational Objectives: The classification of educational goals: Handbook I, Cognitive Domain*. New York: David McKay Co.

Dalton, J., and Smith, D. (1986). *Extending children's special abilities: Strategies for primary classrooms*. Retrieved from http://www.teachers.ash.org.au/researchskills/Dalton.htm.

Gordon, E. (1990). *Centuries of tutoring: A history of alternative education in America and Western Europe*. Lanham, MD: University Press of America.

"Learning objectives: Stems and samples." (2015). *Education Oasis*. Retrieved from http://www.educationoasis.com/instruction/bt/learning_objectives.htm on September 27.

Nyquist, J. (1975). Instructional discussion. Section in J. Stewart and G. D'Angelo's manual *Together: Communicating Interpersonally*. Reading, MA: Addison-Wesley.

Parker, I. (2001). Absolute PowerPoint. *The New Yorker, May 28*. Retrieved from http://www.newyorker.com/magazine/2001/05/28/absolute-powerpoint.

Rowe, M. B. (1987). Wait time: Slowing down may be a way of speeding up. *American Educator, 11*: 38–47.

Wulff, D. H. (1990). Instructional discussion: Planning a discussion. Personal communication.

CHAPTER 12

Conrad, C., and Poole, M.S. (2004). *Strategic organizational communication in a global economy*. Florence, KY: Aldine

DeVito, J. (2008). *The interpersonal communication cook*. New York: Allyn and Bacon.

"Eight Benefits of Online Learning." (2015). *The Association for Supervision and Curriculum Development*. Retrieved fromhttp://www.ascd.org/professional-development/online-learning-benefits.aspxon August 13.

Gibb, J. (1961). Defensive communication. *Journal of Communication*, 11, 1341–1348.

Herold, B. (2015). Why ed tech is not transforming how teachers teach. *Education Week.* Retrieved fromhttp://www.edweek.org/ew/articles/2015/06/11/why-ed-tech-is-not-transforming-how.html.

Mehrabian, A. (2007). *Nonverbal communication.* New York: Aldine.

Smith, P. (2014). Blended learning: It's not the tech, it's how the tech is used. *Huffington Post, November 18.* Retrieved fromhttp://www.huffingtonpost.com/preston-smith-/blended-learning-its-not-b 6165398.html.

Sproull, L., and Kiesler, S. (1994). *Connections: New ways of working in the networked organization.* Cambridge, MA: The MIT Press.

White, K. W., and Weight, B. H. (Eds.) (2000). *The online teaching guide: A handbook of attitudes, strategies, and techniques for the virtual classroom.* Boston, MA: Allyn and Bacon.

About the Author

Ken White holds a B.A. in education from Western Washington University, an M.A. in education, and a Ph.D. from the University of Washington in Speech Communication in the areas of interpersonal, instructional, and organizational communication. He is a tenured faculty member at Everett Community College in Washington State, where he teaches education and public speaking courses. In the 1990s, he assisted the College of Arts and Sciences at the University of Washington to develop and initiate a nationally recognized training program for improving the performance of undergraduate faculty and teaching assistants. Ken consults with local community colleges about training and facilitating the Small Group Instructional Diagnosis (SGID). Besides authoring *Teacher Communication*, he is coeditor with Bob Weight of *The Online Teaching Guide* and with Jason D. Baker of *The Student Guide to Successful Online Learning*. He lives with his wife, Holly, in Washington State.

Index

discussions. *See* instructional
  discussions
dissonance, 101
distances, 24–25
distractors, 56, 94, 107
diversity: communication and, 1;
  confronting, 65; perspective and,
  115
documentation, of communication
  events, 46
Down syndrome, 3
Dreyfus, Herbert, 33
dualistic thinking, 116

Edmodo, 75
email, 51, 74
emotional climate, 114–116
emotions: computing and, 94;
  individuality and, 15; practice
  paraphrasing and, 15; recognizing,
  115–116; relational communication
  and, 21
empathy, 72–73
encoding, 9, 12
ethics, 86
evaluation, 43; of communication
  skills, 43; in instructional discussion
  outlines, 129
expectations, high, 37
experience, 44; sharing, 47
explanations, 17
eye contact, 23

Facebook, 51, 73, 75
facial expressions, 23, 26
feedback, 12; communication
  competence planning and, 45;
  limitations of, 9; message-centered
  model of teacher communication
  and, 9; negative, 19; student, 12–15;
  teachers, 18
feelings: communication of, 102;
  conflict and, 90; of parents, 72–73;
  students and, 33–34
file sharing, 51
five-paragraph outline, 120–122
flaming, 145
focus, in oral presentations, 119
formal positions, 52

forming, 107–108
foundations, 40
fractionating, 95
frameworks, 9
friendliness, 36, 85
fusions of horizons, 62–63, 64

Gadamer, Hans-Georg, 9–11, 58, 59,
  61–62, 65, 83
gatekeepers, 56, 106
gender bias, 66–67
gestures, 23
Gibb, Jack, 143
Gibson, Ted, 22
Girard, Kathryn L., 87
global development delay, 3
goal development, 76
Goldhaber, Gerald, 51
Gordon, Edward, 127
grammar, 16, 141
grapevine, 19–20, 26
ground rules, 115
group work. *See* teamwork
guidelines, 41
gunny sacking, 95

Hall, Edward T., 24
harmonizers, 56, 106
Hart, Rod, 98
Hawthorne effect, 35
Hays, Ellis, 36
Heidegger, Martin, 22, 112
Hellweg, Susan A., 51
hermeneutic understanding, 61
high stakes testing, 1
Holt, John, 134
horizons of experience, 10–11, 11, 12,
  14, 62
house of being, 22
How Children Fail (Holt), 134
Hoyle, John, 83
humanizers, 56, 106
Hurt, H. T., 7

identification, 60
identity construction, 60
imagination, 36
immediacy, 4, 5, 36
individuality, 15